Carolyn &
good to r
& laugh enjoy

THE *Dad* BOOK

Exploring the Role of the Father

DAVID AARON RICHEY

outskirts
press

The Dad Book
Exploring the Role of the Father
All Rights Reserved.
Copyright © 2019 David Aaron Richey
v4.0

The opinions expressed in this manuscript are solely the opinions of the author and do not represent the opinions or thoughts of the publisher. The author has represented and warranted full ownership and/or legal right to publish all the materials in this book.

This book may not be reproduced, transmitted, or stored in whole or in part by any means, including graphic, electronic, or mechanical without the express written consent of the publisher except in the case of brief quotations embodied in critical articles and reviews.

Outskirts Press, Inc.
http://www.outskirtspress.com

ISBN: 978-1-4787-9849-1

Cover designed by James Andrews. All rights reserved - used with permission.

Scripture taken from The New King James Version. (1982) Nashville: Thomas Nelson. All Strong's concordance reference are from: Strong, J. (1995). Enhanced Strong's Lexicon. Woodside Bible Fellowship.

Outskirts Press and the "OP" logo are trademarks belonging to Outskirts Press, Inc.

PRINTED IN THE UNITED STATES OF AMERICA

Dedication Page

This book is dedicated to my children,
their children,
and their children's children.

Testimonials of The Dad Book

Bishop David Richey is a living sermon, a son-father, a father-son. I am beginning to understand why, delivering his consecration message, I felt led by the Holy Spirit to state that David is more than a Bishop...You are about to read a book concerning a matter so holy in God's opinion and written by a loving son-father yielding to the Spirit's inspiration. So holy and of such supreme importance is this business to God that, to avoid striking the earth with a curse, He promised to send Elijah, the prophet, to turn the hearts of the fathers to the children, and the hearts of the children to their fathers. Any neglect of this relationship would be an insult to God's burning concern. In this light, if this book was a father-son relationship laboratory, it would gain a high rating; but it is much more than that: it is a drive to an awareness of the Divine's immediate interest and a crying warning that it must be extremely urgent to us that which is extremely urgent to God, the Heavenly Father.

Archbishop Joseph Joel Laurore
Joel Laurore Ministries
Tulsa, Oklahoma

The Dad Book addresses the importance of the affirmation of the father in the upbringing of a child. Who a child becomes is dictated by the training, instilling, and affirming the father gives during the formative years. How timely in today's society as non traditional families take on the challenge of raising young people.

Bishop Richey writes what he knows but more importantly from the heart of who he is. As a writer, pastor, mentor, and my dad, I cannot think of anyone more qualified to address the need of a return of fathers in the lives of our future generations. This book will be the mouthpiece that will turn the hearts of the father to their children and the heart of the children to their father. (Malachi 4:6a)

Melanie J. Lewis, M.Ed., Ed.S.

I am excited about Bishop David Richey's book on the father's love and fathering. My father died at 41 years of age on April 3, 1956. Losing my father was very difficult for me. My two brothers and my mom and I loved my dad, and it taught me a lesson: We are not promised tomorrow.

David's book talks about our Heavenly Father, earthly father and our spiritual fathers. Some of us only know our earthly father.

When my dad died, I knew on that day that I would see him again in heaven. I knew my Heavenly Father but really didn't understand Him at 11 years old. As I gained age, I reached out to my Heavenly God the Father. I knew He created the world. I knew He created me. I knew He created me for a purpose on this earth. I understood how much He loved me when He sent His Son, Jesus, to die on the cross for my sins.

Since that day in 1956, I was constantly looking for spiritual fathers to sow into my life and affirm me as my dad, Fredrick John Gottfried, did for me. I work with young men without fathers around the United States, and David Richey worked right beside us while beginning our ministry, Team Focus. I tell every young man in Team Focus that God will send spiritual fathers to help us. Our job is to recognize the men that He sends to help guide us. The reverse is true, too. God will send people into our lives for us to help. Our job is to recognize these people as well.

God bless David Richey for writing this book on the father's heart.

Mike Gottfried
Team Focus USA
https://www.teamfocususa.org

TABLE OF CONTENTS

Introduction

WHO IS DAD? Everyone knows who Mom is. There are no ambiguities when it comes to the question of who is Mom. When you see what most would call a great dad, it's as if we want the president to meet him and pin a medal on him, so to speak. With mom, it's the other way around. When you find a not-so-good mom, you'd think the poor lady had committed a sin against God. She's on society's most wanted list. If a dad is raising his kids as a single dad and doing a great job, he gets his own status. Everyone loves him. But there's an unasked question with this dad, "Where's the mother? Why isn't she raising the kid?"

Who is Dad? Our culture seems to be gathering in the boardroom of life to begin to ask the question of what status we should give this other parent. Why can't he just be like the mom and do what he has to do? Why does his job description have so many variations? Is it because he was historically the breadwinner prior to the women's revolution? Do moms have total control now that they are getting more and more equality in the workplace albeit rather slowly.

So who IS Dad? How much influence does he play in the life of an individual? This book explores the position of dad in the life of a human. Great dad, bad dad, no dad, almost great dad, halfway bad dad, this book was designed to be a blessing to all.

Apostle Paul said you have not many fathers. How many is not many? Who are these not many? What do they look like? If you never had a dad, what is the barometer of a dad and especially a good dad? Where does God come into play in the area of Father? Jesus we know, Paul we know, but who is Father God?

This is not a book about fatherlessness but about fathers. It is not about defending wrongs perpetrated against an innocent child. It is more of a text book written by everyone that reads it. This book is your story.

If you are labeled gay, it's your book. If you are labeled fatherless, it's your book. If you had a great dad, it's your book. This book is my book; it's who I have become. I pray that you will enjoy it as much or more as I have enjoyed being the one that presents it to you.

David Aaron Richey,
Dad

$\mathscr{A}$ Message From the Author

On occasion, I've been labeled different things. Growing up, I was the baby. I always hated that label. It sounded like I was a baby. What do babies know? I knew stuff. In the military, guys would say, "He's from Detroit." That one wasn't so bad. But it meant I was bad. I wasn't bad. We moved to Alabama. Everyone knows who I am now. I'm an Alabamian. Let's not mention the black pastor label. Now you know what type of church I pastor. You know what type of service we have. You know we have a choir that sings really well. And you know you will have to bring a lunch so that you will not starve before dismissal. I am not a black pastor.

We like to label people. It helps to describe them when we're talking about them. It fast forwards the relationship thing. "You know who I'm talking about, the black pastor." "Oh, yeah." Instant relationship. Now I know who you are. You're that black pastor. I am not a black pastor. Some of my black friends have labeled me a white pastor. I am not a white pastor.

I noticed another label that I have. It sort of grew on me. So many people call me Dad. Who told them to do that? I didn't. My wife and I are blessed with a ministry called Operation MOBILE. We developed the ministry, but it grew out of her heart. My wife is labeled Mom. She is a mother to the world, literally. It started with a ministry to kids, mostly inner city ages 5-12. I became their dad. That was not the goal. We wanted to teach them the Bible on their level. That is not what happened. We became the Bible.

We began to visit the churches that supported the ministry, and we became their inner city missionaries. However, something else happened. I discovered that many needed a father. All of a sudden, well not that dramatically, but people started calling me their spiritual father. They would tell me that the Lord had spoken to them regarding me. All of a sudden, yeah, I have this label: Dad. But my label is not a label. It's who I am. I didn't know that was who I was. I just became. Without a becoming, I became. It wasn't like I went to college to get a degree in dad-ing. Of course I have five wonderful children, but that's different. Everyone has five wonderful children.

Even my kids are in on this. They've never been envious of sharing me with all of these people. Some of them have become like their biological brothers and sisters. It has been a natural flow in our family. We never had big family discussions about me becoming a dad to the world. It just happened. All of a sudden.

For me, I'd like to imagine myself as the solicitor general that goes before the Supreme Court of the world to defend the dad's position in life. *The Dad Book* is my case that I will present to the Justices. Before entering the court, I know in my heart I have the strongest case ever.

You decide if I'm to win or not.

David Aaron Richey,
Dad

CHAPTER ONE

Daddy WHO?

"DAD, SEE IF you can catch me and you can only swim underwater."

"Got-cha."

"That's no fair you were swimming on top of the water."

"Anna, I'm out of breath. Give me a minute. Listen, take a break. Let me ask you a question: What do you think of when I say the word father?"

"Dad, people think that the father makes the child, but the child makes the father."

"What do you mean by that?"

"A man doesn't become a father until he has a child. The child makes the father."

My youngest and I were having fun in the pool, but the message of "father" was pounding in my thoughts. She was only 12 or 13 at the time, but I like to bounce things off her to hear her response.

When I was a four-year-old boy in my father's house, still tender, and an only child of my mother, he taught me and said, "Lay hold of my words with all your heart; keep my commands and you will live." Proverbs 4:3-4

From the time that Solomon wrote the above passage until now, the role of the father in our culture has changed tremendously, or has it? Let me take you back, even before Solomon. The first act of sin in the Bible was the act of taking the child from the Father. In the first chapters of Genesis we see God and man interacting. Then entering from stage left, Satan also interacts with God's creation. That unauthorized interaction caused man and woman to be banished from their home. Mission accomplished says Satan: broken fellowship of God and mankind.

FATHER IS DEFINED IN THE NEW TESTAMENT ORIGINAL GREEK AS:

generator or male ancestor; the founder of a race or tribe, progenitor of a people, one advanced in years. One who has infused his own spirit into others, who actuates and governs their minds; one who stands in a father's

> Father: one who has infused his own spirit into others, who actuates and governs their minds.

place and looks after another in a paternal way; a title of honor; teachers, as those to whom pupils trace back the knowledge and training they have received. God is called the Father of the stars, the heavenly luminaries, because He is their Creator, Upholder, Ruler.

Anyone who has ever attended Sunday school or read a Gideon Bible in a hotel room can recount the story of Adam and Eve in the book of Genesis.

Genesis 1:27-28 So God created man in his own image, in the image of God created he him; male and female created he them. 28

And God blessed them, and God said unto them, Be fruitful, and multiply, and replenish the earth, and subdue it: and have dominion over the fish of the sea, and over the fowl of the air, and over every living thing that moveth upon the earth.

Satan works hard to kill, steal, and destroy relationships between the father and child. Evil forces target fathers to rid every man, woman, boy, and girl of a relationship with a godly father. So some may say that both parents are important. That would be a correct statement, but for this writing we're looking at fathers. Here's one of the main reasons. Look at part of the definition again:

Father: one who has infused his own spirit into others, who actuates and governs their minds.

The mind is the control center of who we are and who we are to become. The main duty of a father is to teach the child how to think. Thinking determines destiny. Ideally, a father is concerned with the destiny of the child because the child perpetuates the vision of the lineage.

Proverbs 22:6 Train up a child in the way he should go: and when he is old, he will not depart from it.

If the main task of the father is to teach thinking, and the way a person thinks determines their destiny; then the opposition would be to hinder the child from learning the proper way to think. The diabolical reasoning behind stealing fathers is to keep the child from reaching the God-ordained purpose for their life.

The act of training takes time, effort and consistency. The two key words in the above scripture are "train" and "child." Life has intersections, not unlike the meeting of two streets in traffic. These intersections must be navigated to ensure safety and an uninterrupted journey. When a pattern is set during a child's life to discuss the intersections of the day, with a view towards training, the child is taught that their life is a preparation for something.

─╲╎╱─

MELISSA'S BAD DAY

Like most school days, Dad pulls up to the curb in the parent's pick-up zone of Hank Daley Middle School where 11-year-old Melissa is waiting. Richard Bradford owns and runs a business that affords him the opportunity to pick up Melissa after school. Conveniently, his office is only 10 minutes away. Melissa opens the back door of Dad's Tahoe and jumps in the seat slamming it unusually hard.

"Oh, so you don't want to sit up front," Dad says.

"I hate this school!" Melissa yells.

"Excuse me, young lady. Not even a 'Hi Dad, how are you today Dad?' Or how about, 'I think I'll sit in the backseat dad.' What's wrong with you, woman?"

"Dad, I'm sorry. I'm not mad at you. I hate this school. You know I do, this was the worst day of my life. I can never go back to that school again. I can quit school and work for you, Dad. You said someday I'll probably take over the business, so why not start now?"

"Okay, what happened?" Counselor Dad begins.

Richard and his daughter discussed what was disturbing her all the way home. When they arrived at their driveway, they remained in the car like counselor and student oblivious to their surroundings.

─╱╎╲─

What began as the worst day of Melissa's life, evolved into a debriefing of a training operation in the life of an 11-year-old. Richard helped to guide his daughter through the minefield of her day. He showed her how to learn from the minefield, rather than fearing it and never wanting to return. The minefield became her training ground, rather than her demise.

Daddy Richard and daughter Melissa. Now look at King David and son Solomon.

This is not a book about King David and his son Solomon, but it must be noted that it is said of Solomon that he was the wisest man that ever lived. But it must also be noted that David was his father, the one that undoubtedly contributed the most to his wisdom.

1 Samuel 18:14 And David behaved himself wisely in all his ways; and the LORD was with him.

We must further mention that Jesse was David's biological father who taught him to be wise. However, when you talk about David's father, you must mention that God was his father too. Father God taught David more than Jesse! We can see the culmination of all the fathers' teachings, in the wisdom of Solomon. He was one of the richest and wisest men that ever lived!

Have you ever seen the commercials, mostly on late night television trying to get you to buy the greatest invention in the world? The gadget usually cost $19.99. But, when they get to the end of telling you how great it is, they go on and on with, "But wait, there's more." So, let me say, "But wait, there's more."

Ruth 4:13 So Boaz took Ruth and she became his wife; and when he went in to her, the LORD gave her conception, and she bore a son. NKJV

Ruth 4:17 Also the neighbor women gave him a name, saying, "There is a son born to Naomi." And they called his name Obed. He is the father of Jesse, the father of David. NKJV

The richness of Solomon's roots is fully grasped when you read the wonderful story in the Book of Ruth. In the life of Ruth you will see the rich heritage that is culminated in the life of Solomon. The wealth that is in this lineage is a snapshot of what is stolen from a family when the fathers of a line of people are not affirmed.

> Father affirms -builds confidence: trains thinking. Who taught you how to think?

So, when you see Solomon in the Bible you must take into account his lineage: Father God; Boaz (Ruth), Obed, Jesse; David, then Solomon was released with all the foundations that he needed to become, Solomon.

Father affirms -builds confidence: trains thinking. Who taught you how to think?

Solomon's dialogue with God in his dream…

1 Kings 3:9-13 Give therefore thy servant an understanding heart to judge thy people, that I may discern between good and bad… … And the speech pleased the Lord, that Solomon had asked this thing… …… And God said unto him, Because thou hast asked this thing, and hast not asked for thyself long life; neither hast asked riches for thyself, nor hast asked the life of thine enemies; but hast asked for thyself understanding to discern judgment; Behold, I have done according to thy words: lo, I have given thee a wise and an understanding heart; so that there was none like thee before thee, neither after thee shall any arise like unto thee. And I have also given thee that which thou hast not asked, both riches, and honour: so that there shall not be any among the kings like unto thee all thy days.

Solomon learned how to dialogue with Father God. A child must learn how to dialogue with their REAL Dad, Father God, in order to be all that they can be!

> A child must learn how to dialogue with their REAL Dad, Father God, in order to be all that they can be!

_\\\\//_

DAD TEACHES THINKING

As soon as she walked in the door from school you could see it all over her face that something was wrong.

"Hi Dad."

"Hello sweetheart, good to see you."

"Yeah you too; I'm tired. I'm going to my room."

Dad waited a few minutes before knocking lightly on her door, and slowly opening it as though something would jump out.

"So, what's up? What happened?"

"Oh nothing; I'm just tired. It was a hard day, and I went to bed late because I was studying for an exam."

"How'd you do?"

"I think I did pretty well."

"So what's wrong?"

"Okay, you want to know what's wrong? Dad, every time I get on the bus, every time I get off the bus, every time I go to the cafeteria, this girl Debbie is always making smart remarks at me. Dad I'm sick of her; I want to hurt her. I'm tired of this girl."

"So how do you want to handle this?" Dad replied.

"What?"

"How-do-you-want-to-han-dle-it?" Dad mechanically repeats.

"Dad I don't know. You're the one with all the answers, me, I just want to..."

"What?" Dad blurts out, as she mumbles something under her breath. "I didn't hear that," says Dad.

"Nothing"

"Honey who's in control of you? This girl Debbie or you?"

"What do you mean? I'm in control of me."

"If people know they can push your buttons, guess what? They're going to push your buttons. Try to imagine what this kid goes though in her private life if she has to do this to you to make herself feel good. Can you imagine how bad she really feels inside? Who knows what type of home she lives in, what type of parents she has. Does she have anyone to talk to at home? The list goes on. She's probably a very sad and confused young lady. She really needs your prayers. Do not allow anyone to have that much control over your actions. As people of God, we are to be controlled by the Spirit of God, not the Debbies of the world. You got me?

Now tomorrow you know what I suggest you do when she does her little antics?"

"What?"

"Smile at her and say, so how are you today Debbie?"

"Oh Dad, come on!"

"I'm serious, throw her off guard. She won't be expecting it. I'm telling you it'll work." Dad turned to walk out of the room. "I love you, think about it."

"I love you too, thanks Dad."

When dad walked out of the room in the above illustration, the possibilities of chains of thought are endless. Dad planted a seed in his daughter's mind. He gave her another vantage point to consider. Dad gave her an example of how to think.

My wife, Margaret, and I are fortunate to have wonderful children: natural ones as well as spiritual ones. But our youngest biological child, because we were so much older and wiser when she was born, has given me a laboratory of fatherhood. I have incorporated my discoveries into the training and interacting with my spiritual sons and daughters. Because of the similarities in the way she and I were raised, I've been able to revisit the intersections I had with my own parents, especially my dad. I've analyzed what I ought to have learned. I vividly see what I didn't learn. Now, I've been able to develop lessons to teach and help others.

We are both the children of older parents; my parents were about the same age as Margaret and I when Anna was birthed. When I was born,

I was not privy to some of the early struggles that my parents and older siblings had gone through. It was the same with Anna. Around the time

Father affirms - builds
confidence - trains thinking

she was born, Margaret and I started to see more success and blessings in our ministry. Anna was spared from the struggles our older children had experienced.

Father is father. That sounds simple, and it is. Biological father, spiritual father, Father God. Having that strong healthy relationship with a father, assures arrival to your God ordain destiny. Ideally, natural father is there from the beginning to help get you started. If not, there's a plan.

Spiritual fathers are in our lives to build on what our biological fathers began or complete what they started. Spiritual fathers aid or assist if the natural father is still in your life. They also help to repair hurts from any wounds injected by improper fathering. Then there is Father God who is always there.

Father affirms - builds confidence - trains thinking

—ゝ丨╱—

AN EXAMPLE OF DAD BUILDING CONFIDENCE, TEACHING THINKING

"So, what do you guys feel like eating? I think I'll just have a hamburger, its fast."

"Dad you don't need that, it's too fattening."

"Yeah, honey why don't you have a salad?" Mom chimes in.

"Okay, salad it is. Anna, we're going to have dessert?"

"Yes siree Pops."

"Okay, I'll choose this time."

This was a typical interaction with the three of us usually after a full day of ministry. It was done often enough for our daughter to be accustomed to who played which role. She and her mom was there to eat, nothing else. The remainder was taken care of for them.

On one occasion when Margaret and I were out of town, Anna was left with her aunt and older sisters. They had gone out to eat at a restaurant. Anna had her own money and was expected to pay for her meal. This was a first. After all, this was Dad's job, taking care of the check, never discussing cost, prices, totals, etc. On this occasion, limited funds placed her in a new position of looking at the prices on the menu. She later confided: "Dad, I realized, I've never noticed the menu prices."

Matthew 6:26 Look at the birds of the air, for they neither sow nor reap nor gather into barns; yet your heavenly Father feeds them. Are you not of more value than they? NKJV

The task of the natural father is to teach the child in the formative years, the teachings of Jesus found in Matthew chapter six. There is peace and serenity in knowing you always have Dad with you, taking care of all the troubles of life. There is a confidence and faith building process infused into the father/child relationship to propel the child to their God-ordained destiny.

1 Corinthians 4:15-16 For though ye have ten thousand instructors in Christ, yet have ye not many fathers: for in Christ Jesus I have begotten you through the gospel. 16 Wherefore I beseech you, be ye followers of me.

Different fathers, different teachings. There is a connection with a father that you don't have with a teacher. You follow a father; you listen to a teacher. A father, you want to be with; a teacher, you want to hear. It's almost as if each one of us is in a perpetual laboratory, being built into who we are to be for our destiny. Our future changes constantly because we are always changing. We never arrive at a destination off in the wide open yonder, but we are to grow as we are being nurtured into who we are to become. God in His infinite wisdom provides us with the father we need, so that we are fully prepared for what is ahead.

> You follow a father; you listen to a teacher. A father, you want to be with; a teacher, you want to hear.

Because there are so many examples, you must know who your father is and imitate him only. There is to be a certain connecting with your father that ensures a flow of back and forth. The offspring ought to experience reciprocity in the relationship. One of the exciting rewards of being a father is the father receiving from the one being fathered.

You learn to be a father (parent) by serving with a father. Learning to serve; learning to care; learning to father. When you counsel, or pray for someone, oftentimes you receive more than the one being ministered to. In foreign and domestic missions, the joy you experience, usually outweigh what you've given out. With the children you father, more times than not, the same is true. I can say I have received so much more from my children, than I could ever give to them. For those who have not experienced that relationship, it's not something you can fully explain.

Philippians 2:22 But ye know the proof of him, that, as a son with the father, he hath served with me in the gospel.

Growing up as a child, I was probably with my dad more than anyone else if I added up all the time I spent with each person in my life. At the age of seven or eight, I began working with him on a regular basis in his landscaping and lawn care business. Dad was born in Georgia on January 28, 1906; I was born in 1950. So when I was eight, he was 52 years old. These were the days that began my teachings of how a father and son interact my university of son-ship/fatherhood.

Dad was a man that had a bark louder than his bite. Most were afraid of his bark and never got any closer to learn if he would actually bite. I was always around asking questions and poking into his mind. I learned, sometimes the hard way, that he was a great guy. Dad was really a big teddy bear in disguise.

Dad's grandparents raised him, his brothers, and his cousins all boys, on a farm. So the scenario was, a grandfather that dad said was very mean, raising his daughter's boys. Being raised with all boys meant Dad had to learn to fight. My uncle told me once, "You know how some people hit someone and run? Your dad would take two men's heads, butt them together, and walk."

It seemed that Dad was always getting into skirmishes with someone, and I was there supposedly as his backup. This was never discussed, but Dad did not allow too many people to get away with what he thought was an injustice.

Once upon a time, Dad had just purchased a shiny blue 1965 Chevy pick-up. Pulling out of a gas station one day, another vehicle ran into Dad's new truck. Boy was this guy about to have a bad day. Dad jumped out of the truck and looked at the damage. Suddenly without a word, he went over to the vehicle that had hit him, opened the man's door and pulled him out of his car. Dad was about to hit the man with his other fist when a friend who worked at the garage in the gas station, (back in those days you had a one stop service station, where you got your gas and repairs) ran over to Dad, grabbed his arm and said, "Don't hit him Rev, don't hit him

Rev." Did I mention that Dad was a preacher too? Dad's looking bad in this story. Okay, so he had a temper. Okay, okay. A bad temper.

Again, you learn to be a father by serving with a father. Some of the ways I operate in my life is a result of the 1965 Chevy experiences of my life. I always saw dad seemingly not afraid of anything. Nothing. Superman had to take a number and come back next week when it came to my Dad! These were not things that I heard about my father; I was there to experience them.

I probably should have chosen a better example to illustrate Dad's fearlessness. But the blue Chevy one stands out best in my mind's file cabinet. Dad and I, on field trips of dealing with 'wrongs.' Did Dad handle it correctly? No. But Dad was fearless. I witnessed his actions all my formative years. What I gained from it, more importantly, was that God has no fear. God can conquer anything.

It was never spoken to me, but by our relationship, Dad was saying to me, "This is the way you behave as a man." What Dad taught me is what I needed in my call to the nations of the world. I've been blessed to travel to scores and scores of nations, but it began while experiencing life with my father as a boy. Because he showed me how fearlessness operates, I'm now able to go wherever God sends me. I've been able to go into areas of the world where even the natives were afraid to go! I have been into areas where I didn't know if I would come out alive. I've been in a nation where there was fear to just say the name of Jesus, but I spoke His name boldly. I have testimony after testimony of fearlessness being portrayed through me, because the Father had prepared me. How did He prepare me? By allowing me to experience Herbert Richey being fearless. After God filled me with His Spirit, I had a natural example to follow, and a powerful Spirit inside of me to do what God had called me to do.

You learn how to be a man when you are a boy. You learn how to be a father when you become a man. But if you are raised the way God intended us to be reared, you learn both at the same time. That's what a proper relationship with a father imparts.

It is the same with the relationship the daughter has with her father. The daughter is being shown, by her relationship with her father, a paradigm of the way a man is to behave. If there is no father in the daughter's life, then what is her example of how a man behaves?

Once, my youngest and I were on a weekend retreat with fathers and daughters. Every one of the dad-daughter pairs seemed to have good relationships. The youngest daughter was probably 14 and the oldest was about 20-22. It was a relationship enrichment type retreat. We spent the entire three days together doing various exercises to enhance growth in our faith and relationship with each other.

Each of the daughters radiated with confidence; all spoke with boldness, and yet femininity. Each interacted with the other fathers as if they had known them all their lives. It was truly fun to experience.

It was a joy to behold as we did the trust fall. Each member of the team, dads and daughters alike, positioned themselves on the edge of a platform. It was approximately four feet high. The candidate was instructed to turn their back to the team, which was on the ground. They were equally spread out, facing each other, with their arms pointed towards the person they were facing. The team was excited and prepared to catch the person on the platform, as they fell backwards into the arms of their team.

I described the scene because each young lady, as she took her position on the platform, showed absolutely no fear. She simply walked to the edge of the platform, turned her back to the team on the ground, and fell back into our waiting arms.

The coach of this particular exercise exclaimed that she had never seen a group as confident, totally showing no fear at all, as our group had exhibited.

> *Ephesians 6:4 And, ye fathers, provoke not your children to wrath: but bring them up in the nurture and admonition of the Lord.*

The main focus of the father is for the child to arrive at this place of confidence and trust in order to be all that God intended for them to be.

The father's task is to remain focused on the vision for their children or the child may get frustrated. Fathers must keep the child focused on trusting him during this stage or they may lose the student/child's attention.

Ephesians 6:4 And, ye fathers, provoke not your children to wrath: but bring them up in the nurture and admonition of the Lord.

It is a balancing act of the father to build confidence, without breaking the spirit of the child. When the spirit of the child is broken, he/she will probably lose focus on what is being taught. Once a father loses a child's focus, it is difficult to regain it.

Colossians 3:21 Fathers, provoke not your children to anger, lest they be discouraged.

Hebrews 12:9-11 Furthermore, we have had human fathers who corrected us, and we paid them respect. Shall we not much more readily be in subjection to the Father of spirits and live? 10 For they indeed for a few days chastened us as seemed best to them, but He for our profit, that we may be partakers of His holiness. 11 Now no chastening seems to be joyful for the present, but painful; nevertheless, afterward it yields the peaceable fruit of righteousness to those who have been trained by it.

Correction is not just for correction's sake, it's for training. So, in order for the correction to be complete, it must be walked through and not merely meted out. This part of the father's job is extremely important. The main reason it must be learned, is that God will follow this same principle to secure holiness and achieve destiny. Others in authority throughout the life of an individual, with different management styles, will dole out correction too.

When the child/student is made to focus on the leadership style of the father/mentor, it takes away from the lesson to be learned. When the emphasis is on the leadership style of the father, the environment

> The father needs to discipline himself where he is cognizant of every interaction with the son or daughter,

is conditioned to stimulate emotions rather than mind and spirit. The child then develops the habit of dealing with training and correction emotionally. This trait is carried over into the relationship with Father God. The father needs to discipline himself where he is cognizant of every interaction with the son or daughter, especially where discipline is involved. Remember the father trains, and affirms. Discipline is the strongest tool he uses. He must mirror Father God when disciplining his son or daughter. Father God waits until the right moment for discipline. He knows how strong of an impression the discipline imparts upon His son or daughter.

Fathers govern your mind (thought process). What you are going through? How is it affecting you? What are you learning as you are walking through life?

Destiny is a funny thing; you don't arrive you become. You discover destiny that God has already built for you. Because there are so many variables in life, as stated before, it's as if we're in a perpetual laboratory.

Who wants to sign up to be in a laboratory? Right? No one. Hence, the struggle of becoming. Ideally, Dad removes the struggle and replaces it with encouragement and assistance.

> Fathers govern your mind (thought process). What you are going through? How is it affecting you? What are you learning as you are walking through life?

There is to be a certain connecting with your father that ensures a flow of back and forth. The offspring ought to experience reciprocity in the relationship. One of the exciting rewards of being a father is the father receiving from the one being fathered.

It's not that we cannot learn how to be a father from other sources, it's God's perfect plan that we learn from our father. Certainly many have gone on to be great fathers, never having had a true example to follow. But there is another certainty too, there is a void for father, in the heart of the fatherless.

—◈—

GRANDPA'S TEACHABLE MOMENT

Recently I had the lovable assignment of taking my six-year-old granddaughter to school. It was a cold wintry morning. As is my custom, I checked the weather by opening the weather app on my phone. As is her custom, she watches every move I make. We briefly discussed the weather of the day and what we both were wearing, then I placed my phone on the counter. Susie, (that's my nickname for all my girls,) begin to navigate through the app while waiting for me to finish making my to-go coffee. Grandpa was silent of the phone indiscretion; I picked it up and we walked to the garage to leave. Upon arriving at her school, the normal routine is to wait in line until school opens with all the scores of other moms, dads, and grandparents dropping off their cargo.

This is our grandpa/granddaughter time to bond while discussing various topics. This morning, as she crawled across the console between the two seats to sit in the seat across from me, she did something she's never done before. Why did she do it today? I've taken her to school 222 times, yet she's never done that before. She adjusted the power operated multiple positioned seat. Without asking nonetheless. Grandpa had two indiscretions to discuss. I did it in a teaching mode, not a condemning mode. It went something like this,

"Gracelynn, remember this morning how we discussed the weather?"

"Yes sir, I remember."

"I placed my phone on the counter after I checked the weather. You picked it up and began to look through it, right?"

"Yes, Grandpa," probably thinking to herself, *okay where's he going with this? He looked at the phone to find out what the weather was, I did the same. I hope I'm not in trouble.*

"Whose phone is it?

"Grandpa, it's your phone."

"Do you think you should have asked me if you may look at it?"

"Yes sir." *Oh, I see where he's going with this. I hope he doesn't say, don't touch my phone again. I just looked at it and maybe a few other things, he wasn't using it. It was just sitting there! I didn't think that was wrong. He's let me look at it before. What'd*

I do wrong? God, talk to my grandfather please! she probably thought.

"Now, just a minute ago," Grandpa continues his debriefing, "when you jumped up front, you adjusted the power seat. Did I say that you could adjust the seat?"

"No sir," she said sheepishly. "Sorry, Grandpa."

"No I don't want you to be sorry, I just want to teach you something. One of the things we have to learn in life is to respect other people's belongings. Do you know what respect means?"

"Maybe, no."

"Just as you have things that belong to you and you only, others do also. Treat others as you want them to treat you. You respect the other person's belongings, by letting them know that you know it belong to them. However, if you would like to use it, you ask them. If they say no it's okay, if they say yes, be grateful and say thank you. Because after all, it doesn't belong to you, it belongs to them. You get it Susie?"

"Yes sir, sorry Grandpa."

"No no, you're an amazing young lady, Grandpa simply want you to be the best you that you can be. When I teach you, it's not because you're bad, but because we're making you better."

A few moments passed and then,

"Grandpa you're the best grandpa any girl could ever have."

Ah man, did she have to say that? Sure sounds good though.

She is a sensitive child and deserves my respect and carefully chosen words to correct, teach, and educate. I want her to learn submission, not oppression. I think I did okay.

Hebrews 13:17 Obey them that have the rule over you, and submit yourselves: for they watch for your souls, as they that must give account, that they may do it with joy, and not with grief: for that is unprofitable for you.

The above word SUBMIT, in the original Greek manuscript means: To resist no longer, but to give way, yield. To yield to authority and admonition, to submit

The father needs to discipline himself where he is cognizant of every interaction with the son or daughter, especially where discipline

> Submission is an attitude, not an act.

is involved. Remember the father trains, and affirms. Discipline is the strongest tool he uses. He must mirror Father God when disciplining his son or daughter. Father God waits until the right moment for discipline. He knows how strong of an impression the discipline imparts upon His son or daughter.

Submission is an attitude, not an act. Because submission is best learned during training, few grasp the full understanding- simply because of lack of father/child training.

The main reason of Jesus' coming was to bring us back to the Father. Jesus spoke throughout His time on earth of His relationship with the Father. There are so many biblical references, too numerous to mention of the relationship of Jesus and God the Father. Jesus taught how to relate to the Father. Jesus was God manifested in the flesh, yet He humbled Himself, yielding to His Father, during His time on earth. Submission is such a necessary teaching because it clothes an individual with a key attribute needed to be successful in relationships. We have a major problem, nearly insurmountable, in our world today because few are willing to yield or submit. They see submission as weak, when it actually shows strength.

JULIE'S NIGHTMARE FATHER'S DAY

Julie was not satisfied with her mom's explanation of why Dad deserted her and her mom. She knew her dad was on drugs, but it never really hurt their relationship. Mom said it was another woman. Dad didn't have another woman. Did he? No way!

One Friday before Father's Day, Julie came home from school to find her mom sitting on the sofa with her face wet with tears. You could tell by her face and the look that this was really bad. "Mom, what's wrong?" Julie asked. "Nothing." "Mom are you serious? Nothing is your answer? "Your dad's gone." "Gone? Gone where? He's coming back right? MOM, he's coming back right? MOM?"

That Father's Day weekend was the weekend Julie died for the next seventeen years. For seventeen years Julie hated, and dreaded Father's Day like it was the plague. A Christian counselor along with the great man that Julie married finally got her through Father's Day.

Think about this for a moment. The most important relationship in your life, is all of a sudden gone, and you had no input regarding it. Your trainer, your coach, your mentor, gone and no one debriefs you regarding the circumstances. You are left to your own thoughts, emotions, and yes, deep pain. This scenario occurs thousands, probably millions of times in homes across the planet. In our illustration our subject was healed, albeit seventeen years later. How many are never healed? How will they survive?

If you didn't grow up with your dad, what are your thoughts on Father's Day?

LET THE HEALING BEGIN

The following are Healing Questions you may want to ponder alone or with someone you trust:

1. If you do not have a father in your life, why not, and how does it make you feel?

2. Are there thoughts about your biological father that you need to say out loud?

3. Do you need to forgive a father who is currently in your life?

4. Do you need to forgive a father who is no longer in your life?

5. If you have a father in your life, do you properly appreciate what he brings/adds to your life?

CHAPTER TWO
Your DNA Test

"DAD, can I go with you?"

"No."

Dad and mom are discussing the business as they always do at this point, so I know what's about to happen. Dad owns a small landscape and lawn care business. Mom is preparing statements for customers that Dad hand delivers to collect. This is an all-afternoon trip with stops for sodas, bathrooms, and possibly a restaurant or bakery. This is not work, this is heaven on earth on a Saturday afternoon. It's been long enough, time to try again.

"Dad can I go with you?"

"I told you no!"

Mom's almost finished. The list is made out in the order of stops. The statements are completed with envelopes stacked and ready. This is my last chance. He's about to walk out the door. He's taken me on several occasions before, what's so different today?

My plan usually works, it's well thought out. I ask. And Dad says, "Yeah, come on." We jump into the car and travel together. Simple. I know all the fun he's going to have. I love being with him. Dear Lord, I hope he lets me go. Okay, okay this is it. This is the third time, this is going to make or break me. "Dad, can I go?" No answer, he just looks at me with that, "are you still on that question that's already been answered," look?

So I follow him out the door. He gets in the car, starts the engine. To him, I'm not on the planet. He totally ignores me as he puts the car in reverse to back out of the driveway. It's probably a 100-150 feet driveway. I move to the middle of the driveway with sadness knocking at my emotional door. I don't have time to answer the door because dad is in the street about to put the gear in drive.

Suddenly, an act of God. I didn't hear any music, but this is the part in a movie where the heavens open up. He leans out of the car window and motions his hand for me to come. I run down the driveway faster than an Olympic track star. I jump into the front seat with gleam in my heart. I dare not smile or gloat. This is not a winner/loser deal. We both understand that this is a win-win situation. He's a busy man. I'm nine or ten years old. He's got work to do. I want the goodies and the thrill of being with him. He loves me, but he could probably get things done faster and easier without a little person hanging on. I love him so much. "Come on." I can still hear those words.

Throughout the Bible we observe Father God's tremendous love for His children. He placed that same DNA in mankind. But in many men that trait has not been able to flourish because of the programming the man-child received regarding being a father. A boy is not simply a boy but a man-child. A girl is not merely a girl, but a woman-child. How does a man-child learn to lovingly provide, to lovingly correct? We've heard time and time again how the man is to be tough and hard. Yet we expect him to be able to train his tender little offsprings. Being a man is not synonymous with being tough and mean. If God were tough and mean with His people, He wouldn't have many people! If biological father didn't teach in a tenderly fashion, spiritual father must fill in that void, or the person may find themselves in the bull-in-the-china-shop scenario more times than not.

It is God's original plan for nothing to compare with the passion that a father has for his child: watching the child grow, learning new things. That's the pride of the father. The child's failures are opportunities for a classroom teacher/pupil tutoring. They are not looked upon by the father with discrediting eyes. A father waits to see the child's response to the failure and how it will help or hurt their journey to their destiny. He also patiently waits for the son/daughter to come and discuss the failure. Rarely will the father bring it up in an accusatory way, but instead hope that they will bring the matter to him for counsel.

⁓

TAKE IT TO DAD

"Dad, I got fired today."

"What happened? Why did they let you go?"

"My boss said the company was downsizing, but Dad, he never liked me from the beginning."

"Oh come on, don't look at it that way. Let me ask you, did you learn anything while you were there?"

"Yeah, never think you'll be at a job for long if the boss doesn't like you."

"Seriously, what do you have now, that you didn't have before you were hired there?"

"Well, I guess I did get some experience in managing people. I certainly learned more about computers. Hey, maybe you're right Dad. I guess it's not all that bad, huh?"

"See what I mean? Seek the Lord for something better. He has something better for you. The glass is half full not half empty."

"You're okay Dad. I think I'm going to keep you around."

"Thanks a lot. I was worried there for a minute."

The above illustration was a learned interaction. The son learned early in life that Dad was there for him. He learned that just like a backboard of the basketball hoop, Dad is there to help get the ball through the ring. You still have to pick the ball up and shoot it towards the ring, but Dad is the backboard. When you learn this process, you take it throughout your life. They are debriefing intersections of the journey to better explain the next intersection.

You may be saying to yourself: you don't understand how I was raised. My dad was not there for me. Or, I never knew my dad. I grew up with my dad coming home drunk every night and beating me and my brother. Maybe you're thinking thoughts like, I could hear my mother in the next room begging my dad to leave her alone. My mom had to get up at 4:30 to go to work, but he was too drunk to care.

When you've grown up under circumstances such as those, it may be difficult to conceive how a loving father would want to be there for you unconditionally. Naturally your DNA does not change, but spiritually it can. The need arises for new spiritual DNA. Then, you will not respond to life's experiences the way the former dysfunctional programming wired you to respond. The best way for that to occur is a healthy relationship with a spiritual dad, which will give you a paradigm of a loving dad.

Proverbs 22:6 Train up a child in the way he should go, And when he is old he will not depart from it. NKJV

Remember, a dad trains. So, a dad trains the child in the way he should go. After you've trained the child, you can comfortably release that child to their Real Dad, Father God. The questions that everyone has will already be answered: Who is Father God? What does He want from me? Why am I on the planet? Where am I headed and how will I know when I get there? All those questions and more are answered during training.

The most important part of being a human is to know and understand the heart of the Father. Our total being hinges on that knowledge and understanding.

God created us for a reason; no one is a mistake. He told Adam and Eve to be fruitful and multiply. After the flood, He told Noah and his family to do the same. The reason for those commands is so that YOU may come forth!

Hop over to the book of Jeremiah and take a look:

I can just imagine little Jeremiah before he became the prophet that we all love and respect. He came from what we would say today, a line of preachers. So, it was expected that he too would be of the same order.

But at the time of his call, God knew he needed a bit more than just, "Jeremiah, I need you to go to work." What God did in his call was to give us a glimpse of how intricately involved He is in the life and destiny of a person.

Jeremiah 1:4–5 Then the word of the LORD came to me, saying: 5 "Before I formed you in the womb I knew you; Before you were born I sanctified you; I ordained you a prophet to the nations."

In the passage: Before I formed you in the womb I knew you, the word "knew" is the same word used to describe the intimate relations experienced by a husband and wife.

From the millisecond the seed meets the egg, God is involved in the life of the person! The providential care that He has over our life is nothing short of amazing. If all the i's and t's of a person's life are not dotted and crossed, God has a plan. When the person finally says yes to the will of the Creator, a spiritual father is made available to help get the person back on track.

The great question of mankind is, "How do I get to the purpose that I was created for?" The answer is in the relationship with the father.

WHAT IS YOUR SPIRITUAL DNA?

I don't have a lot of scientific knowledge of DNA (deoxyribonucleic acid). To simplify it for me, I learned from TV crime shows that if I come upon a crime scene, don't touch anything. That's all I need to know about DNA. But to get a working knowledge, I researched and learned that it is the major component of chromosomes and carries genetic information. It is amazing the intricate detail in which God made the human being. DNA is self-replicating and is responsible for passing along hereditary characteristics from one generation to the next. Research shows that our natural DNA is tied to a numbering system in our chromosomes, 23 pairs which equals 46. I believe that God has a divine order for our destiny, and it is in your spiritual chromosomes. Let's say that our spiritual DNA is: Divinely Numerically Activated.

> The great question of mankind is, "How do I get to the purpose that I was created for?" The answer is in the relationship with the father.

Your natural DNA says whether you will have big feet or a little nose. Spiritual DNA says where you will take those big feet and little nose. Natural DNA has to do with characteristics, spiritual DNA has to do with character. Your spiritual DNA says how you will behave in any given situation.

It is interesting how a child will look like one parent or the other. Sometimes a generation will be skipped and the child will look like the grandparents or an uncle or aunt. Brothers and sisters may or may not look like each other. In many cases, they don't even resemble one another. The opposite of that is true too. They may not be twins yet look exactly alike.

That is true in the spiritual realm too. When you are in the presence of the spiritual father absorbing, something is happening. After a while that person becomes a part of you. You begin to talk, think, and behave exactly like that person. Because it is spiritual and not natural, you may receive and become something that the father hasn't received or become.

"You are the same today as you'll be in five years except for two things: the books you read and the people you meet." Charlie "Tremendous" Jones

The world did not receive Jesus until He became a son through a relationship with Father God and a relationship with His earthly father Joseph.

Isaiah 9:6a For unto us a child is born, unto us a son is given……..

We can clearly see in the following scripture that Jesus thought He was ready for His call at twelve years old.

Luke 2:44-49 but supposing Him to have been in the company, they went a day's journey, and sought Him among their relatives and acquaintances. 45 So when they did not find Him, they returned to Jerusalem, seeking Him. 46 Now so it was that after three days they found Him in the temple, sitting in the midst of the teachers, both listening to them and asking them questions. 47 And all who heard Him were astonished at His understanding and answers. 48 So when they saw Him, they were amazed; and His mother said to Him, "Son, why have You done this to us? Look, Your father and I have sought You anxiously." 49 And He said to them, "Why did you seek Me? Did you not know that I must be about My Father's business?"

> We are all children of God, but we are not all sons of God. Son-ship denotes relationship.

JOSEPH WAS A FATHER TOO

The Bible does not state this; however, it is implied that Joseph taught Jesus some things that no one else could have taught Him. As a carpenter, it was a process to take a raw piece of wood and make it into something beautiful and useful.

First, he had to find a live tree and chop it down, causing it to die. Needless to say, he couldn't use anything that was still alive. After chopping it down, causing it to die to self so to speak, he began to clean it by removing parts of the wood, like the bark or limbs or knobs. After cleaning it, he began to make it into whatever the vision was for that piece of wood. It may have been connected to another piece to make a bigger or more useful item. Maybe it was molded and shaped into something that would be a vessel to carry or hold something.

$$\sim \!\! \prime \! \backslash \! \sim$$

What kinds of things do you think Jesus encountered during His first thirty years of being a person on earth? Jesus had to relate like you and I in order to become Jesus, the Son of God. You are called by your name until you become what you are called. That is why it is so important to have the proper words enter into your mind. The words that you hear are used to help make you into what you are to become. The job of the father is to ensure that the child is not called something that he/she is not to become. Once the wrong words are engrained into the psyche, it requires effort to make corrections.

In my global travels, I have observed that the name of a newborn is usually tied to something. The name of the child has a meaning associated with destiny, the day they were born, their lineage, tribe, and so on. So when you call that person's name, you are speaking more than just what they are called. If you call someone something long enough, they will become what you are calling them.

Other scripture confirms what occurs when you are mentored or fathered. Take Romans 8:14, For as many as are led by the Spirit of God, they are the sons of God. We are all children of God, but we are not all sons of God. Son-ship denotes relationship.

The same holds true for your natural father. He may have provided the seed, but after that act, he had no relationship with you. You may have not had a simple conversation with him your entire life. A famous radio personality correctly calls that type of dad a sperm donor. So naturally, you're his child but not his son or daughter. No relationship.

During the season that I met my wife I was fasting almost constantly. Prior to that, I was eating everything I could get my hands on. I loved baking all types of sweets. Most times I would eat the entire thing in a few days. As a result, I had a lot of impurities in my body. As I began to fast, the impurities started to surface in the form of boils all over my body.

I looked malnourished. But that didn't stop that beautiful creature from heaven from falling in love with me. She was definitely in love with my spiritual DNA more than my natural DNA.

Within four months, we were married and began our journey of becoming one. This is where it gets interesting. After years of marriage, I began to look like her naturally. What is even more interesting, she began to look like me spiritually.

THE PASTOR'S SPIRITUAL DNA

I was invited to preach at a church where I barely knew the pastor. As I entered the church for the first time, a woman greeted me and smiled as if the smile was painted on her face. Each member handed me off to the next helper until finally I arrived at the pastor's office. I noticed that each member of the church acted exactly alike, as if it had been rehearsed. As I pondered this short episode, I could see each member of the ministry behaving as their pastor behaved toward me. Everyone that I encountered in the ministry was behaving like their pastor. They had his spiritual DNA.

It is so important that we are around the people that God has ordained for us to interact with, or we may receive the wrong spiritual DNA. And, there are two sides to that coin too. We want our spiritual father's DNA when it's the proper one chosen by God Himself.

In a perfect world, we would all have the nice little family that we see in the movies the ones where they are all living happily ever after without any problems. But this is not a perfect world. Since the fall of man in the Garden of Eden, there has been a fight against the position of the father. God as well as Satan knows that if you don't have a strong paradigm of an earthly father, it is very difficult to unconditionally receive your Heavenly Father.

One may say, my father was never there for me my entire life. The goal of Satan is for that person to not have faith in God's ability to do what He says He will do. That person may not articulate it, but their actions will show that they struggle in the faith area. If Dad was cruel and harsh toward a child, that grown up child may think of God as a punisher. They may see God as One waiting for them to sin, in order to drop the hammer on their head.

Because there are so many examples, you must know who your spiritual father is and imitate only him.

Let's go back to 1 Corinthians 4:14-16

I write not these things to shame you, but as my beloved sons I warn you. 15 For though ye have ten thousand instructors in Christ, yet have ye not many fathers: for in Christ Jesus I have begotten you through the gospel. 16 Wherefore I beseech you, be ye followers of me.

The New International Version makes it a little clearer: For in Christ Jesus I became your father *through the gospel*. (Italics mine)

So, Paul is saying in this passage: Me, the Word, and the Holy Spirit, caused you to BE. Since that is the case: Therefore I urge you to *imitate me*. (Italics mine)

Paul, as spiritual father, is saying in essence: I need for you to realize how your spiritual destiny came into existence. Once realized, get involved and imitate your father. Because it is your spiritual DNA and not your natural DNA, you have an option of not agreeing with the Spirit. You DO NOT HAVE TO cooperate.

I have to say repeatedly: different fathers, different teachings/ anointing. There is a connection with a father that you don't necessarily have with a teacher. You follow a father, you listen to a teacher. You want to be with a father, you want to get information from a teacher.

Jesus was God's only begotten Son, but you are to be begotten too. By whom?

> There is a connection with a father that you don't necessarily have with a teacher.

God has a vision for your life. That's why God chooses a spiritual father, so that you may be a begotten son/daughter too. There is a certain spiritual DNA that God desires for you to have inside of you. So, this spiritual father is selected, handpicked by God. Just any ole Tom, Dick or Harry dad will not due. (Okay, so that probably was not the best expression to use in this type of book.)

Our relationship with Father God is enhanced when we have a good healthy example of a relationship with an earthly father. Just as there was a reason for Jesus being begotten, the same holds true for you and me. Ideally, a father has a vision for his child.

Look at the word BEGOTTEN in the Greek, the original biblical manuscript of 1 Corinthians 4,

It comes from the words gennao and ginomai: be born, gender, bring forth, of men who fathered children; to be born; to be begotten; of women giving birth to children; metaphorically: cause to arise, excite; in a Jewish sense, of one who brings others over to his way of life, of God making Christ his son; of God making men his sons through faith in Christ's work, offspring, to become, i.e. to come into existence, begin to be, appear in history, come upon the stage; of men appearing in public; to be made, finished.

I purposefully used many of the synonyms the *Strong's Concordance* gave, yet I did not exhaust the list. All these meanings are clothed in emotions revealing the importance of coming into existence via the chosen spiritual father handpicked by Father God.

Through the gospel, I have caused you to rise.

Through the gospel, I have excited you.

Through the gospel, I have caused you to come upon the stage.

Through the gospel ...... The list is numerous because God uses the Scriptures to form His people.

In Genesis 1:26, we see the Godhead making a decision to: Let us make man in our own image.

Just like it took a triune to make the first man, it also takes a triune to make you.

Because man is so important and the destiny so sure, God must ensure that the right signature (DNA) comes together. The right father, the right word, being properly led by the Holy Spirit of the Living God.

Yes, the father has the vision, but you must have the word for proper growth and forming.

You must be led by the Spirit to know when, where, and how.

There is certain knowledge of the word of God that your particular spiritual father has, and you need. The manner in which that spiritual father delivers that word. The experiences that the spiritual father has, OF that word, that is special for each son and daughter. All these components work in tandem to produce an awesome offspring.

> *2 Timothy 2:15 Study to shew thyself approved unto God, a work-*
> *man that needeth not to be ashamed, rightly dividing the word of*
> *truth.*

That is why one must study to show themselves approved unto God rightly dividing the Word. God prepares one to be a father and then sends those to the spiritual father. The father is encouraged by God to prepare, in order to have the proper word, for the ones that will be sent.

Just as in the beginning, God said let us make man in our own image. Here's how He says it today: let us make spiritual man in the image of his/ her spiritual father whom He has chosen for you, coupled with the Word and the Spirit of God.

To produce in the natural you need three: a male, a female, and the womb. To produce in the spirit you need three: spiritual father, the Word, and the Holy Spirit, a replica of the Godhead in the beginning.

WHAT OTHER AUTHORS ARE SAYING REGARDING THE INDELIBLE MARKS A FATHER MAKES ON HIS CHILD:

According to John Drescher, our children need our time. He encourages parents to take time "to listen to a child's concerns, drop the newspaper when he speaks, look into his eyes when he talks to us." He tells this story of a son needing the attention of his father: A small boy watched his father polish the car. He asked, "Dad, your car's worth a lot, isn't it?" "Yes," his dad replied, "It cost a lot. It pays to take care of it. When I trade the car in, it will be worth more if I take care of it." After some silence the son said, "Dad, I guess I'm not worth very much, am I?"

When spiritual fathers spend time with their sons, their sons know they are worth a great deal in the fathers' eyes. A father knows that when he invests his life in nurturing his son, the son will grow up to be spiritually productive. A father will experience the joys of fathering when he takes what he has and imparts it to others. To impart means to give to another what one is/has. Through a spiritual father's teaching and influence, an impartation is conferred to his spiritual son. (p. 41 from "The Cry for Spiritual Fathers & Mothers" by Larry Kreider)

J.B Phillips quote:

We want, in fact, not so much a Father in heaven as a grandfather in heaven – senile benevolence who, as they say, "liked to see young people enjoying themselves" and whose plan for the universe was simply that it might be truly said at the end of each day, "a good time was had by all."

LET THE HEALING BEGIN

The following are Healing Questions you may want to ponder alone or with someone you trust:

1. Is there something in your natural DNA that seems to hinder you from being all that you are to be?

2. Recall some of your natural responses to life's intersections that point you back to your natural father. Do those responses cause you to think ill or well of your natural father?

3. Reconcile any character traits in your DNA that you have a disdain for, that you can trace back to your natural father.

4. If you can identify your spiritual DNA, what does it look like? And who is the spiritual father?

5. Have you given thanks for the blessings you have received from any spiritual father that you have had or is currently in your life?

CHAPTER THREE
Formed OR JUST BORN?

THEY HAD BEEN watching each other every Sunday across the congregation. He had been divorced for more than two years and she was a single mom. Many times, they would catch the other looking with a smile. Lisa had been thinking, "I wonder if he likes me. He sure is cute." Terrance would think to himself, "I know what the pastor preaches but this woman is so fine. She might not be wife material, but I would like to get close to her." One Sunday after church, Lisa got the nerve to walk up to Terrance and speak. She asked him if he would like to go get something to eat. After all, her mom had the children for the weekend and she didn't know what she was going to do for dinner. Terrance's heart jumped. He quickly said, "Yeah sure." He was embarrassed by his rapid response. They laughed and agreed on where to meet. Driving out of the church parking lot Lisa thought, "Now this is only dinner girl, nothing else." As Terrance followed her out of the parking lot, he wondered, "How far is this going to go? What am I doing, Lord?" After three hours at the restaurant, Lisa asked Terrance if he wanted to go back to her house for coffee. Again, Terrance's words seemed to be out of his mouth before he spoke, "Yeah sure." They arrived at Lisa's house. Walking up to the house, Terrance could feel his heart pounding as if each step were getting him closer to some sort of doom, yet he was excited by this mix of emotions. It was an anxious "what am I doing" kind of thing. As they sat on the sofa Terrance built up enough nerve to touch Lisa's hand. He met no resistance. He pulled Lisa close to him and began to passionately kiss her. They began to quickly undress each other as if the fastest contestant would win a prize. Lisa led Terrance to her bedroom where they began to consummate what had started weeks ago in the church sanctuary. After they finished their act, they both fell on their backs in unison and thought to themselves: "What have we done?" They were ashamed to look at each other as Terrance slowly got up and quickly dressed. He walked out of the house with not a single word spoken between the two, as a man walking to prison's death row.

Can you imagine how many times this scenario happens? This act would forever change both characters' lives. It all began with a thought that was generated by the way each of their characters were formed.

—◦╲╿╱◦—

TERRANCE'S BACKGROUND

Terrance joined the church months before with a desire to change. He wanted something better. He grew up with his parents breaking up and getting back together year after year. He later found out that his mom learned of his dad's infidelity and put him out of the house. After some time, he began coming around and before long he had moved back in only to rehearse the same old song after a few months. Terrance decided that when he grew up, he would never be like his dad. But upon entering high school he found himself going from girl to girl, tiring of each one after only a few dates. After high school, he went into the Army where he met what seemed to be his soul mate, Monique. After a short whirlwind-dating period, they were married. About a year into the marriage, Terrance could not believe that he found himself following the same pattern his dad followed all his life. When the ugly divorce was final, Terrance promised himself that this would never happen again. "Women are no good," he told himself. *(The story and characters have been created from years of counseling and do not represent any individuals present or past.)*

LISA'S BACKGROUND

Twenty-eight-year-old Lisa is an unwed mother of three. All the children were conceived by different fathers, and she has never married. Lisa never met her father. He left her mother soon after she was born. She thinks he is in prison but there have been no attempts of contact with him or any of his family. Her mother will not speak of him and has brushed off any references that Lisa has made of him over the years. Her babies' daddies all fit the same mold: single, nicely dressed, handsome, with a mixture of a shy aggressive personality. Each relationship followed the same pattern. Lisa would meet each man and the relationship would immediately become sexual. Each relationship ended once it was discovered that Lisa was pregnant. The pattern was always the same: infrequency of coming around, fewer phone calls, unanswered text messages, excuses, and finally a disappearance. Lisa always told herself that she had learned her lesson only to find herself in the same scenario after months or even a year or two of no dating. Lisa worked her way through school, holding up to two jobs at one time. She finally completed her education. She went on to work as a computer analyst in a growing company. Desiring more and longing for a relationship with God, Lisa began visiting churches along with her three children. Finally, she joined a church that she and her children really enjoyed. Lisa soon became very active in the church, volunteering in several departments. Then, the daily routine of life, job, home, children, church and mortgage became overwhelming. She started staying home on Sundays just to try and get some rest. After a while she began going back to church but not with the same frequency and fervor; something was different. Lisa would go to church maybe one or two Sundays a month. Then she met Terrance and... *(The story and characters have been created from years of counseling and do not represent any individuals past or present.)*

Just as someone can be abnormally formed in the natural, one can also be abnormally formed spiritually. The behavior of the characters in our story above was obviously improper, but the root cause was their abnormal forming.

We were formed-good or bad.

We're being formed-good or bad.

We must be formed-to achieve our destiny that God has ordained for us.

From conception, man is in a continual process of being formed.

WE WERE FORMED

Think of the human mind as a computer hard drive that retains everything that is keyed into it. God made our brain to retain everything it encounters. That's a good thing, but it can also work against us. Some things we want to forget but are always thinking about. Others we want to remember but forget. Being formed by the experiences of life is similar to a file on a computer. You may not be able to locate the file without endless searching, but suddenly there it is!

Amazing. It was there all along. Or the file may be easy to locate, and you are able to identify and open it at will. You may delete a file and think it's gone forever, but the computer geeks have told me, that given the right circumstances you can restore even those files. Once we become born again, it is necessary to reprogram this computer.

> *2 Corinthians 5:17 Therefore if any man be in Christ, he is a new creature: old things are passed away; behold, all things are become new.*

I love this scripture; however, this is a spiritual concept that must be walked out into reality. The characters in our illustrative story above were formed. They didn't come into the world knowing how to behave in the manner depicted in our story.

WE ARE BEING FORMED

You've undoubtedly heard someone make the statement of being in a rut. How did that person get in the rut? The building of a rut begins with the pouring of the foundation of a thought. The thought naturally flows into an action that is repeated. It culminates with a habit that receives the label of a rut. That's why we must be cautious of the ones we befriend. We need to know who are our children hanging out with because they are all being used to program their mental computer.

We may get something on our hard drive that we don't want. We may allow a virus to enter our spiritual hard drive and cause our computer to crash. A process of forming may begin with a sermon from the pastor on Sunday. It may be an inspiring book that changed your life. But then you go to work on Monday and you forget everything by listening to those that are anointed by the devil to steal your destiny.

From Chapter two: "You are the same today as you'll be in five years except for two things: the books you read and the people you meet." Charlie "Tremendous" Jones

If you desire to direct your forming, you must direct your input. The task of a parent is to guard a child's input. However, it does not end with childhood; it begins at childhood and never ends.

If our natural father was not in our life or didn't provide the necessary input, then it creates a larger task for the spiritual father. If our natural father was in our life and did a great job of forming us, that's fine. However, unless that father can continue to father at the pace necessary for healthy spiritual growth, you will need a spiritual father to come alongside. The spiritual father receives the baton to then continue to provide nourishment. The ideal circumstance will provide an environment to grow step by step into a blossoming state of glory to glory. Many are left in a hanging in midair state. Fatherhood requires the father to continuously pour into the child. When that flow is missing, the child's growth is stunted. That father/child relationship is to be like a thriving plant in a tropical paradise.

WE MUST BE FORMED

We've looked at this before. When young Jesus was in the temple with the priest at the age of twelve, He thought He was formed and ought to be about His Father's business. But Joseph and Mary took Him back home with them for another eighteen years.

Luke 2:51-52 And he went down with them, and came to Nazareth, and was subject unto them: but his mother kept all these sayings in her heart. 52 And Jesus increased in wisdom and stature, and in favour with God and man.

Jesus spent thirty years privately being formed for three years of public ministry. Why would we be any different? Jesus increased in wisdom, stature, and favor with God and man. Young Jesus experienced God's ideal parenting program. He was taught by His earthly parents and Father God.

Jesus grew as a child the way God intended all of us to grow having two earthly parents, following the plan of God for our life, and for the lives of our children. Then, at the appropriate time, we release our offspring in the way they should go. This well-trained

> Jesus spent thirty years privately being formed for three years of public ministry. Why would we be any different?

child then follows in the path set before him/her. In a perfect world, that is the way God intended for it to work. However, the norm many times is best summed in Galatians 4:19,

My little children, of whom I travail in birth again until Christ be formed in you,

Most parents desire for their children to first, grow up. Secondly, get an education and acquire employment that will place them on a path to success. Then, if they desire, marry, buy a house, and live happily ever after. However, forming encompasses the total person the thought processes, personality, emotional maturity and the ability to make proper life choices. If there has not been a concerted effort on the part of the parents and especially the father, to form that person for their destiny, it's very possible there will be complications later on.

God has provided a sort of safety net by giving spiritual fathers to His children. Coaches, bandleaders, bosses etc., can provide mentoring. This cannot be discounted. But for the total person, there must be a forming of the spiritual man by a trained spiritual father.

When a person comes to a spiritual father, there is an unspoken assessment of the needs of the new son/daughter. The father must be willing to go the distance to see him/her formed in the way God ordained, so that they may reach their destiny.

If the need is there, this is where travail in birth again comes into play,

Galatians 4:19 My little children, of whom I travail in birth again until Christ be formed in you,

As a spiritual father, you take great joy in the ones who come to you and immediately begin to shine. They look as though they receive everything that is imparted to them. They seem to grow in maturity with not so much as a hint of heartache. Then, there are the ones on the up and down graph. They will have it one day, only to lose it on another day. This is not etched in stone, but eventually one of two things happen: Something will click and they are on their way to success, and all that God has for them! Or, they will continue the roller coaster of life until, well, everyone is different.

For the ones that get it, it is a joy to see them arrive at the different plateaus of their journey. For others, it is heartbreaking to see their potential, and then watch as they continue to struggle with the same problems and situations.

There are different reasons why one would need to be formed again, but the process is the same.

Again, the main job of the father is to teach the child how to think. Thinking determines destiny. To change destiny, you must change thinking. Reprogramming our mind is equivalent to a woman delivering a baby. Okay, so moms would probably say that's a stretch, but it is extremely difficult.

Take sports for example. Many times, the coach will encounter resistance while teaching a player a technique that is contrary to what they have already learned. In the same manner, we struggle to change our learned behavior after seeing our parents behave a certain way. It is difficult to change that paradigm. The thinking is struggling with an already learned habit of the mind and body.

So, many do not reach their destiny because they are not prepared for it. They're not formed. I'm using the biblical term formed, but it could be interchangeable with the words: mentored; programmed; affirmed; or discipled.

> Again, the main job of the father is to teach the child how to think. Thinking determines destiny. To change destiny, you must change thinking.

Inside of you are dreams and visions that point to why you were created. Because a great God created you, there is greatness inside of you. It is God's original plan for parents to realize the potential in their child, then nudge and encourage him/her to that destiny. However, because of lack of parental training or more importantly the lack of fathers, many come to the table of life with less than adequate skills. Many overcome those obstacles and rise to the top either in spite of the lack, or because of it. Yet, others die, never arriving at the purpose they were created for.

⁓

EXAMPLE OF FORM - CHELSEA - FUTURE CLOTHES DESIGNER

Frank and Marie ended their marriage when Chelsea was nine years old. No one ever told Chelsea the cause for the nasty divorce. She later found out through the family gossip line that her dad had an affair with a woman from his job. Her mom found out about it and even caught them together one evening at the local coffee shop. Chelsea reasoned that her dad slowly stopped spending time with her because the other woman had children. After a while, she rarely heard from him.

Chelsea began spending more and more time alone. Her mom worked and she was an only child. Chelsea had a passion for clothes. As a little girl, she would dress her dolls in different fashions she designed. Little Chelsea would have fashion shows with her models and buyers from around the world. She redesigned her dolls clothes to her taste, taking old tee shirts and socks and made them into designer fashions from different countries. Chelsea spent hours with her imaginary fashion shows.

As Chelsea got older, she was the fashionable trendsetter among her friends. But another dynamic was occurring at the same time. Every time Chelsea would come up with a new trend, she would hear snickering and mockery from her peers and little encouragement. After enduring the mockery for as long as she could take it, Chelsea resorted to looking like everyone else. But after a while, she would discover another style they certainly would accept.

Chelsea noticed, that soon after she stopped wearing her trendy outfits, the girls that mocked her, began wearing her invented trends. She also noticed that no one laughed at them. In fact, they were given credit for coming up with an awesome outfit. This happened over and over again until Chelsea stopped her trend setting. Chelsea later became known for her less than attractive clothes. Even though Chelsea had become a very attractive woman, you couldn't tell it. She now wore unattractive clothes with outdated bifocals hanging on her nose. Chelsea never married or had children. She lived a secluded life. It all began as a little person, playing with dolls.

⁓⁓

No one was there for Chelsea to encourage her. There was no one to cheer her on to her destiny. No one told her how good she looked or how creative she was. During the times the girls made fun of Chelsea, no one was there to help process the pain of rejection and hurt. As a result, the dream of greatness died inside of her.

EXAMPLE OF FORM - LET'S BUILD A CASTLE!

Once upon a time, while walking on the beach enjoying the sun in my own little world, I came upon a small group of children working feverishly to create their version of a castle. They were using their buckets of sand mixed with the proper amounts of water as if they were commissioned to form King Arthur's castle. One child seemed to have the main task of running back and forth to the ocean delivering buckets of water. He'd dumped the water into a holding area near the building site. Then the other workers conveniently filled their buckets as they continued to form their structure. As I came closer and closer to this group of pretenders, I steadily watched and analyzed their movements.

I began to think of the word form. All through our life this term is used by us and on us. Form a sentence. Form a line. In what form will you present it? Form an opinion. As often as this term is used in life, how many think of it as a process that is used on each one of us to create a finely crafted vessel in whatever sphere we are called to? Of course, we don't want to concentrate our forming to the sandy beaches of a summer vacation. But the forming of one's life must be explained in the terms of building structures in order to fully understand the need for experienced God-ordained engineering for our destiny.

Matthew 7:26-27 And every one that heareth these sayings of mine, and doeth them not, shall be likened unto a foolish man, which built his house upon the sand: 27 And the rain descended, and the floods came, and the winds blew, and beat upon that house; and it fell: and great was the fall of it.

In the beginning God formed, then created us to form too.

We see examples throughout the Old and New Testament of form. In Genesis 2:7, the Lord God formed man. In Jeremiah 18, God gave the prophet a metaphoric example of what He wanted to do with Israel by forming them like a potter forms clay. In Romans 12:2, Paul encourages the readers to be transformed: it's a Greek word metamorphoo. It's where we get our word *metamorphosis* from. It's best understood in the changing of the tadpole to a frog or a caterpillar to a butterfly. So, you may

> In the beginning God formed, then created us to form too.

be the tadpole, but a spiritual father helps you to become a frog. That doesn't sound too good. You were the caterpillar; spiritual father helps you to become the butterfly! How's that?

FORMING AND REFORMING

Genesis 2:7 And the LORD God formed man of the dust of the ground, and breathed into his nostrils the breath of life; and man became a living soul.

Jeremiah 18:3 Then I went down to the potter's house, and, behold, he wrought a work on the wheels. 4 And the vessel that he made of clay was marred in the hand of the potter: so he made it again another vessel, as seemed good to the potter to make it.

In Jeremiah, there was a reforming because the original forming was marred.

Marred: - corrupt, battered, to destroy, go to ruin, decay; to be spoiled, be corrupted, be injured, be ruined, be rotted; ruin; to pervert, corrupt (morally).

If one's forming process results in an abnormal form, a need is created to go through a reforming process to correct the abnormality.

The synonyms of marred help to explain the intense need for guidance in order to be made whole again. Dad's position on the court of life is to guard and protect you before you become corrupt and battered. But if life's rough experiences cause decay,

> A father has the most honored position from the Maker to affirm the child and endorse who they are as a son or daughter.

rot, or ruin, then God's perfect plan is to have a spiritual dad there for the reforming process.

To pervert, is another synonym for marred. It is to use something incorrectly or improperly. This is probably the saddest expression of the forming process. When a creation of God is perverted from what it was intended to be, it is the highest form of being marred and in dire need of reformation.

It also proves the case of the need of the father to affirm and to teach the child from the beginning of his or her life as to who and what they are. A father has the most honored position from the Maker to affirm the child and endorse who they are as a son or daughter. It is the paramount need of the offspring to hear their entire life:

You are an awesome son.

You are beloved my daughter.

Son, you are growing into a fine young man.

Daughter, I am so proud of you. Your beauty is astounding.

Daughter, your mother and I love you so much.

Those imprints into a boy or girl are the primary groundwork and building blocks to forming and pointing them to their God created destiny.

Being marred is not the end, there's hope.

> From conception, man is in a continual process of being formed.

We were formed-good or bad.

We're being formed-good or bad.

We must be formed-to achieve our destiny that God has ordained for us.

From conception, man is in a continual process of being formed. Experiences of life can easily get us off track and present a need for reforming. It is not hard to get marred as we walk along life's highway. We are in this world, born in sin and shaped in iniquity. However, it is difficult to reach the totality of your destiny abnormally formed.

_\\|/_

VICTORIA'S SECRET

Victoria's father, Jackson, was a merchant marine. He was away from the family months at a time. During the months he was home, Victoria thought he detested her because he had almost no interaction with her; and when he did, it was always in anger. Victoria remembers vividly one experience with her dad that scarred her for life. When Victoria woke up that morning, a sense of fear overtook her. Her eyes began to focus on the new day that was bursting through her window. Suddenly, her mind collided with the thought: "Daddy's coming home today. Oh my God."

Victoria realized she hated Saturdays. They took away safe hours that her time at school afforded her. Her mom rose early preparing for the arrival. Mom was all over the place cleaning, rearranging, throwing out, and picking up things. She almost forgot to iron Dad's clothes! He had to have everything ironed and folded or he threw a fit. Jackson usually arrived in the early afternoon with the ship getting into dock early morning.

This day was different. Victoria walked down the stairs and spotted her father through the sheer curtains on the front door walking up the stairs of the porch. She remembers the time on the clock on the wall: 8:25 a.m.

Victoria's heart stopped and never seemed to start back up as she froze on the stairs. The old wooden porch and the quiet Saturday morning announced Jackson's early arrival like a scene in a suspense movie. Every sound in the house stopped as his key turned the lock on the door.

Victoria jetted back up the steps and slammed the door of her bedroom. She paced back and forth replaying the horror films of her past dysfunctional encounters with her dad. Victoria could hear the muffled sound of her parents beginning to argue in a question/answer tone. Her father's voice grew louder and louder, and her mother's responses were less frequent. Then it happened. Her dad called out her name seemingly with the volume of a policeman's bullhorn: "VICTORIA! Get down here, now!"

"Oh my God" feared Victoria. "What have I done?"

Victoria ran down the stairs as fast as her feet would carry her, so as not to anger her father any more than he apparently was. "Why are you not down here helping your mother?" Jackson yelled at Victoria. Before she could speak, he began hitting and slapping her as hard as he could with the front and back of his open hand while calling her every name that entered his deranged mind. Victoria's mom pounced on his back and began choking him. Jackson tried to get his wife off his back by swinging his body back and forth in an agitator washing machine motion. Jackson swung at Victoria hitting and missing as she began dodging the blows. Suddenly, everyone fell to the ground, knocking Victoria's head on a glass table. She was cut, bruised, and knocked unconscious. The 13-year-old awoke later that evening in the hospital with her mom at the edge of her bed. Neither one spoke of the incident that day, and Victoria never saw her father again.

There may be a drastic difference between your personal experience of a father and the biblical definition. Do not allow any dysfunctional

Father Affirms - Builds Confidence - Trains Thinking

definition of a father you may have had in the past hinder you from receiving the healing that comes from the warmth of the love of the Father.

Let's recall the biblical definition,

Father, Pater- generator or male ancestor; the founder of a race or tribe, progenitor of a people, forefather. The authors of a family or society of persons animated by the same spirit as himself; one who has infused his own spirit into others, who actuates and governs their minds; one who stands in a father's place and looks after another in a paternal way; a title of honor; teachers, as those to whom pupils trace back the knowledge and training they have received; God is called the Father of the stars, the heavenly luminaries, because He is their Creator, Upholder, Ruler.

Father Affirms - Builds Confidence - Trains Thinking

The Father has a plan to restore the father/child relationship,

Malachi 4:5-6 Behold, I will send you Elijah the prophet before the coming of the great and dreadful day of the LORD: 6 And he shall turn the heart of the fathers to the children, and the heart of the children to their fathers, lest I come and smite the earth with a curse. KJV

Luke 1:17 And he will go on before the Lord, in the spirit and power of Elijah, to turn the hearts of the fathers to their children and the disobedient to the wisdom of the righteous—to make ready a people prepared for the Lord." NIV

There has been much discussion on the timing of the fulfillment of the above scriptures. Will Elijah return? Was John the Baptist a fulfillment of the scripture because he came in the spirit and power of Elijah? Regardless of one's interpretation, it is the will of Father God to turn the hearts of fathers to children and the hearts of children to fathers, because each needs the other.

John the Baptist prepared the way for the Lord to come by preaching, "Repent for the Kingdom of Heaven is at hand." When Jesus came on the scene, He too began to preach the same message and included a clear way back to the Father.

I never searched for any of the spiritual fathers I've had in my life, including the one I have now. It just happened. That may sound strange, but I believe because I had my dad in my life growing up and I understand fatherhood, God always provided someone to coach me at different junctures.

At this time in my life, I'm what you would call a low maintenance son. There have been times when I'm sure I dominated my dad's time, but it paid off in the long run.

We talked about this scripture in Chapter One,

1 Corinthians 4:15 For though ye have ten thousand instructors in Christ, yet have ye not many fathers: for in Christ Jesus I have begotten you through the gospel. 16 Wherefore I beseech you, be ye followers of me. KJV

NIV: 16 Therefore I urge you to imitate me.

You will require different fathers in your life to provide the necessary forming and reforming needed for your advancement. As a person gets older, it requires different teaching methods than when one is younger. The father that God has for you will need the skills particular to your personality and character. Recognize him when he's in your life or you'll miss the needed forming that they are sent to impart.

STRONG HEALTHY RELATIONSHIP WITH FATHER

Strong Healthy Relationship: *A mutual association based on each partner giving freely and receiving willingly what each one brings to the relationship. Both partners wanting the best for the other's growth, enhancement, and well-being.*

The awful spirit of destroying relationships in general, and father/child relationships in particular, has been in the world since the beginning. But God always has a plan. When Jesus began His earthly ministry, He immediately began to speak of returning to the Father. Jesus always pointed to His relationship with the Father. He truly came to restore the relationship of the child with the Father.

Life can be so harsh and cruel many times, until a person will think that the best plan of action is to avoid any resemblance of the past trauma at all cost. That holds true of a relationship with a father too when the relationship may have been unbearable. Or at best, one may say, I've done pretty good without a father, I can go on with my life without one. But that is not God's plan. God has a father waiting for you. Open your heart to receive, if that's you.

> The awful spirit of destroying relationships in general and father/child relationships in particular, has been in the world since the beginning.

Daniel 11:32b but the people that do know their God shall be strong, and do exploits.

This scripture can also be applied to your natural or spiritual dad. It means to know by experience. Some things are caught rather than taught with just hanging around dad. There is a forming process occurring that you are not aware of because of the ease and gentleness of the practice. For those that have not had that all their life, when God brings that relationship into their life it requires effort to get accustomed to it. It is Father God's desire that you enjoy the peace and security of a strong healthy relationship with a natural dad and/or spiritual dad. That relationship feeds into the growth it affords with your relationship with your Real Dad, Father God. The relationship with a father carries reciprocity. The dad is receiving the joy and admiration of watching an offspring grow and bring forth healthy fruit. The only payment due is the open gratitude of the child.

LET THE HEALING BEGIN

This Chapter has a more extensive healing section. Take whatever time needed to go over it alone or with someone you trust. You may want or need to revisit this section more than once.

Acknowledge the pain. IT HURTS.

Don't spiritualize the pain and pretend the hurt, wounds and suffering do not exist. Facing that hurt will become a bridge to the destiny God has ordained for your life. Experiences, situations, and circumstances, are field trips on the journey to your destiny. They help to build you into a better child in the kingdom of God.

Our reactions to those actions afford us an opportunity to respond like God's Word tells us to respond, or they provide evidence that we need a little more grooming.

Don't minimize the pain. Understand it.

Proverbs 3:13 Happy is the man that findeth wisdom, and the man that getteth understanding.

Proverbs 4:7 Wisdom is the principal thing; therefore get wisdom: and with all thy getting get understanding. KJV

Where did your father learn to be a father? Where did his father learn to be a father? Who taught your father how to think? The behavior that he conveyed to you, or is conveying (if he is still in your life) is learned behavior. I'm not excusing any of the improper acts but merely creating an atmosphere for releasing. The umbilical cord of your suffering must be cut, so that you can breathe on your own.

FORGIVENESS

Part of the healing process is to forgive the father that left you behind or the spiritual father that didn't understand your need for healing. Whatever dysfunctional father/child relationships you've had in the past, don't allow it to hinder you from progressing. The runway to your healing is forgiveness.

Matthew 6:14-15 For if you forgive men when they sin against you, your heavenly Father will also forgive you. 15 But if you do not forgive men their sins, your Father will not forgive your sins. NIV

Matthew 5:44-48 But I say unto you, Love your enemies, bless them that curse you, do good to them that hate you, and pray for them which despitefully use you, and persecute you; 45 That ye may be the children of your Father which is in heaven: for he maketh his sun to rise on the evil and on the good, and sendeth rain on the just and on the unjust. 46 For if ye love them which love you, what reward have ye? do not even the publicans the same? 47 And if ye salute your brethren only, what do ye more than others? Do not even the publicans so? 48 Be ye therefore perfect, even as your Father which is in heaven is perfect. KJV

Life has ups, downs, curves, and cliffs. Even though some of them may seem unbearable, they can be used to make one a better traveler on life's highway. And if we learn from each jolt, we may even arrive at our destiny intact. Everything about our life should point us to Father God and make us more like Him. Learning to walk in a healthy relationship with an earthly father, serves to enhance our relationship with our heavenly Father and other relationships in our life as well.

> Unforgiveness binds like the shackles of a prisoner

UNFORGIVENESS BINDS LIKE THE SHACKLES OF A PRISONER

Unforgiveness is holding someone or something captive in your heart. The memory burns your soul, creating spiritual sores that fester from time to time throughout your life. Over time the bruise is covered with a scab, only to flare up again when that sore is hit with a similar blow or old memory. Release the person or the experience. Even though it's not an easy task, it can be if you desire it enough.

Matthew 18:18 "I tell you the truth, whatever you bind on earth will be bound in heaven, and whatever you loose on earth will be loosed in heaven.

This scripture is speaking of someone that has offended you. It is extremely important that you release them for your healing to begin. Release them by asking God to help you to love them. Release them by forgiving them. When you begin to do this, you may have to do it simply out of obedience. It may begin with your teeth clenched together. But soon it will become a part of your heart. When they are released from the clutches of your pain, healing will begin. You'll be free from the shackles of the past to soar into your destiny.

BECOME CONNECTED TO YOUR FATHER

When sin entered the world, its first act was to separate the offspring from its Creator. Satan couldn't destroy the Creator or the offspring, so he destroyed their relationship. His goal was to separate the offspring from the Father, thereby handicapping the child and creating unhealthy growth. God was vehement in His statement to Adam and Eve: "Who told you, you were naked?"

Genesis 3:11 And he said, "Who told you that you were naked? Have you eaten from the tree that I commanded you not to eat from?" NIV

Meaning: "You're my child. I'm the one that formed you. Who, other than Me, have you gotten information from?"

I cannot emphasize enough the importance of having the father in your life, regardless of your age or where you are in life's journey. Being connected, not acquainted or affiliated, but connected with a father, adds volumes to developing momentum to soar into your destiny.

CHAPTER FOUR

YOU ARE NOT A PRODUCT OF YOUR ENVIRONMENT

ONCE UPON A time in the gym that I frequent, I was drawn away from my time on the elliptical. Instead of listening to the music blaring through my MP3, I began watching one of the twelve televisions on the wall. I quickly understood it was not because I had heard the same music on my MP3 over and over. I was drawn to a talk show with a guest that was discussing a topic dear to my heart.

"Today on our program we have Jennifer, who says she is a man trapped in a woman's body. Jennifer is planning to cut off her breast, change her name to Conrad, and live as a man. Her mother and two aunts are with her, and they say she is wrong for doing this and are begging her not to disfigure her body in this way. One of her aunts says if Jennifer would only say yes to Jesus she would be changed and would not want this operation.

Her aunt further says if Jennifer does this she will burn in Hell. When we return after a short break, we will talk to this family about Jennifer's proposed half transsexual operation. We'll be right back."

> It takes a male and a female to produce an offspring. What is the male's part in this process and what is the female's part?

As I'm listening to this program, I'm waiting to hear the whereabouts of the father. It's finally revealed, almost in passing. Okay, now we're getting to the heart of the matter, I thought. It was not addressed. It was as if no one even mentioned the dad. The aunt said, "She has been angry at her dad." However, she just threw out this statement with a list of other things Jennifer was upset about. The aunt was describing Jennifer's attitude and behavior, not the absence of her father. The father was never brought up again the entire program. "Hey guys, is anyone listening?" I wanted to scream out. "The lack of affirmation by the father." To the Jennifers of the world, can we talk for a moment?

It takes a male and a female to produce an offspring. What is the male's part in this process and what is the female's part? I'm not talking physiologically, but what are the actual roles of each parent in the life of their child? When is the offspring released to be and/or to do as he or she will? How does this offspring arrive at this releasing?

For 40 weeks, a little person is formed in Mom's womb. All concerned are wondering what it's going to be. Is it a girl? Is it a boy? Speaking of a boy and a girl, I recently learned one of my spiritual granddaughters gave birth to her second set of twins a girl and a boy! What are they going to look like? Whose nose will the girl have? How tall will they grow to be? The questions are endless. I have two granddaughters that live near us. It's rare that I don't see them every week, and I thank God for that. I'm in a constant state of watching them being formed. The four-year-old (the four-and-a-half year old, as she doesn't fail to remind us) does not look like she did three years ago. I love the way her personality is forming. Her vocabulary has become very large for her age. I must admit, I was concerned about the development of her speech and vocabulary. Those fears are completely gone now that her verbiage has formed. From conception the baby begins a perpetual process of being formed.

So, how *is* a person's sexuality formed? Can we simply say a person's genitals tell us their sexual orientation? With homosexuality as rampant as it is in the world, are we to look further than between the legs? I think so. Homosexuality didn't just begin; it's been around for as long as people have been on the planet. Just as the parent is concerned about the proper forming of their child, shouldn't we teach forming of sexuality too?

The pregnant mom is surrounded by warnings of what to do and what not to do. It's as if the mom takes second place in the care department and the little person is number one. Everyone is saying, "Be careful, you know you're pregnant. You can't eat that. You can't do this, that, and the other thing, you know you're pregnant! You don't want to affect the baby's forming," they will say. What about the little person's sexuality? Are we to mention that during and after pregnancy? Is that to be left to chance or to genitals? I think not. When the little person begins to form in the womb, or when he/she is delivered, everyone's curious of what the genitals will reveal. It's universal. Once the sex is revealed, the attention is focused on forming the remainder of the little person, never to mention the sexuality again.

~ゝ◦ー

MARTHA'S MOVE TO HALLSBERRY HIGH SCHOOL

She was so angry at her parents for getting a divorce. But on the other hand, Martha was relieved the fighting was over. Mart, as everyone called her, was distraught at the thought of leaving her beloved sanctuary, George Butler High. To start a new school in the middle of the semester was insane! She begged her mom to allow her to remain at Butler and live with her aunt until she graduated. Her mom said it was too close to her dad's job; it was out of the question.

Mart and her mom walked down the hallway of Hallsberry High towards the admin office. She felt as if she had been tried and convicted of a crime she did not commit. Now, she was being transferred to a maximum security prison to begin her eighteen-month sentence! Mart sat in the waiting area while her mom went in to talk with the assistant principal. For a reason unknown to Martha, her mom wanted to talk to the principal in private.

On cue, as Martha's mom entered the administrator's office, a student entered the office and plopped down in the seat next to her.

"Whasup?"

"Hi."

"You go here?"

"No. Yeah."

"Which one? You know where you go to school, right?"

Martha giggled at herself for being totally out of character. She began to feel like she was talking to a cute boy and felt weird that she liked it. Her new interviewer was certainly a female but dressed like a male. Her hair was cut short, and her short-sleeved uniform polo had the sleeves rolled up. If not for the C cup shirt, the person on her right would definitely be a boy. A cute boy.

Mart never discovered what her mom and the principal discussed. But her mom stayed in the office long enough for the chance encounter to produce friends. JJ and Mart exchanged cell phone numbers. They discovered that both lived alone with their moms. JJ never met her dad. Mart hated her dad. JJ was gay. Mart was interested. When Martha's mom finally came out of the office, Mart had decided that she really liked her new school.

The two girls quickly became besties. They spent countless hours together in school, overnight stays, and weekends. Martha's mom was relieved that she had settled in so quickly and found a friend to keep her occupied. After all, with all that she had to be concerned with, at least she didn't have to worry about Mart. As for JJ, her mom was consumed in her job and rarely had time with JJ. She was an only child and her only grandparents lived hundreds of miles away. JJ rarely saw them.

Mart embraced her new life, feeling at ease to dress and act like her lover. But the girls parted ways almost as quickly as it began. Even though they entered into new relationships with other girls, they continued to be friends, laughing and comparing notes often.

Both girls, in our imaginary story, were not affirmed by their dad. There's danger when the father does not affirm the child in their sexuality. The child is left with a void in their thinking towards their sexuality. That void is then filled by an endless number of sources. On many occasions, there is a saving grace of a strong technical thinking mother that is able to fill in like a dad. When that is missing, the child can move into same-sex sexuality. Even if the person never actually operates in homosexuality, the potential is there.

I've heard it said many times, "My dad was in my life and I'm gay." This confirms it does not negate the importance of father. What this statement says, is that my father was in my life but he didn't affirm me. How many have experienced people in their life, yet they do not know anything about the person? The dad may have been living in the same house, but he wasn't there socially. The dad may have been there, but his interaction with the child was not affirming but condemning. The dad may have lived in the home, but he did not interact with the child in their love language. (We'll talk more about this later.) There needs to be a reciprocating loving relationship between the father and child. Those are the ideal ingredients to ensure the production of an affirmed child.

> The role of a mother is the same throughout the life of the offspring: NURTURER. The role of the father throughout the life of the offspring: PROVIDER.

Let's repeat:

Since our conception we are in a constant state of being formed.

We have been formed-good or bad.

We are being formed-good or bad.

We must be formed-in order to achieve our destiny that God has ordained for us.

The role of a mother is the same throughout the life of the offspring: NURTURER.

The role of the father throughout the life of the offspring: PROVIDER.

Proverbs 13:22a A good man leaves an inheritance to his children's children,

According to this scripture, a man is still providing for his children long after he's left the earth.

The mother's womb and body is designed to nourish the embryo from the moment of conception. If allowed, the mother continues to provide nourishment, regardless of how old her child lives to be. Everyone knows at least one man called a momma's boy. The duration of the father's role is similar. He provides the sperm. Yet, he is expected to continue to provide for the child long after he is no longer on the planet. The man is designed to be technical in his pursuit of providing for his child and family. Proverbs 13:22a says, "A good man leaves an inheritance to his children's children,"

MOM -NURTURER – DAD -PROVIDER

The dad is to build and form the child to BE a provider. A provider for him/herself. Now, of course the parents work in tandem to build their child. This is not to minimize the role of the mother. However, until recent years it has been the fathers who have been absent, not mothers. Absent fathers have caused the rampant growth of devastating statistics of families. And let me go on record to say, it is absent fathers who on a large scale have caused the out of control rise in the statistics of homosexuality. The unconfirmed stats that I have found for single parent home are: In 1950 the percentage of Black children born in single parent homes were 6%. The current statistics are an alarming 72%. Couple that with the flooding of homosexuality in our communities at large. It doesn't take a very smart person to connect the dots.

Again, let's focus on the biblical definition of father, not on any dysfunctional experience of father that someone may have been exposed to.

Father as defined in the New Testament original Greek:

> A father affirms - builds confidence- trains thinking.

Generator or male ancestor; the founder of a race or tribe, progenitor of a people, one advanced in years. One who has infused his own spirit into others, who actuates and governs their minds; one who stands in a father's place and looks after another in a paternal way; a title of honour; teachers, as those to whom pupils trace back the knowledge and training they have received; God is called the Father of the stars, the heavenly luminaries, because He is their Creator, Upholder, Ruler.

A father affirms - builds confidence- trains thinking.

Let's discuss methods of forming

We discussed in Chapter One the force of evil that has existed since the beginning of time to steal fathers. The reason there is a demonic spiritual bounty on the father is simple. The main role of the father is to form the child's thinking. That includes thinking toward their sexuality too. Why would God make us with brains to think and not have a vision for us to be taught how to think?

Colossians 3:21 Fathers, provoke not your children to anger, lest they be discouraged.

This verse does not address parents or mothers with the warning "provoke not," but specifically fathers. The role of the father is not merely to discipline for incorrect thinking but to train and encourage proper thinking. It is the same manner Father God teaches through His Word (law), through the teachings of teachers, and our environment. All three methods of forming are designed to ensure the child (person) arrives at the destiny ordained for them.

Again, some have said their father was in their life during childhood and they are gay. I cannot overemphasize that just being there is not enough. Dr. Gary Chapman's five love languages properly answers this question. His book titled, *The Five Love Languages*, describes in detail each love language and their pros and cons. When you interact with anyone, you achieve more by using and understanding their love language. For example, the child's

> Remember, the job of the father is to affirm. How difficult is it to affirm when you are not connected? Virtually impossible.

love language may be words of affirmation, and the father is harsh with his words. The child's love language may be quality time, and the father is always absent. And that's just naming two of the five. There's much more to it than my simple example. If the father does not have an understanding of the child's love language in his interacting with him/her, it's difficult to teach thinking. Why? Simply because the parent is not getting through. How many times have you been turned off by someone because it seemed like they didn't love/like you?

> *"People don't care how much you know until they know how much you care."*
>
> — Theodore Roosevelt

If the father doesn't connect with the child, it's difficult for the child to receive from the father. Relationship denotes connection. Remember, the job of the father is to affirm. How difficult is it to affirm when you are not connected? Virtually impossible.

Most people love the way they want to be loved. Let's add to that statement: Most fathers affirm their children the way they want to be affirmed, or the way they were taught to affirm. In most cases this is instinctive. There is no discussion with the child by the parent such as:

"Now, Johnny, your mother and I are going to love you in this manner so that we may affirm you." No one talks to their child like a science teacher.

We interact in the same manner that God interacts with us. We are formed by our dad with the same tools that God uses to form us. God uses His spoken word and His written Word, the Bible. The natural father and spiritual father in like manner use words.

Father God uses teachers to form us. Those teachers may or may not teach in the manner that is conducive for us to learn. But they teach nonetheless. Again, our natural father and spiritual father teach us. Also, their manner of teaching may or may not be conducive for us to learn.

Lastly, God uses our environment to teach us. The root of the word environ, says surround. Whatever surrounds us, good or bad, leaves an impression on us. However, we can learn from both. Good or bad

> In order to be a good leader we must first learn to be a good follower. A leader follows vision.

environments surround us. The $64,000 question is, how does a good or bad environment form us? Just as Father God uses our environment to form us, so does our natural and spiritual father.

Since people are part of our environment, they play a large role in our forming. How we end up on the path of life depends largely on the skill level of the natural and/or spiritual father. I know that's a lot of weight on the dad, but the responsibility clearly lies on him.

I'm attempting to paint a picture of what can happen if, say, the natural or spiritual father does not have the knowledge to properly form the offspring. Much time is wasted by being with the wrong teacher. What occurs in the forming, when the instructor is teaching false and/or wrong teachings? What is the result of one's forming, after being with a teacher that programs the psyche with junk that requires years to overcome?

The original plan of God is to have the child walk along life with the parents, until it is time to be released. Ideally, the parents will follow God and His Word in raising the child. The result: When the child is on its own, it will continue to follow in the path he or she was taught.

THE DAD TEACHES FOLLOWERSHIP

A leader is a follower. Parents, and especially the father, must train in follower-ship. We will follow something or someone our entire life. In order to be a good leader, we must first learn to be a good follower. A leader follows vision. When you take your eyes off the vision, you're distracted from your

> Connection is to produce power not weakness.

goal or destiny. The objective of the enemy or opposition is to get you off focus, so that you will not achieve your goal. The role of the father is to form and discipline your thinking. Then, you will know who you are and why you're on the planet. The father's goal is for you to have the skills to remain, not simply arrive. The by-product of this training is that you learn follower-ship. Then, you are well qualified to follow your Real Dad, Father God.

Spiritual fathers are not only for those who did not grow up with their natural dad. The role of the father doesn't decrease because we grow older, become more mature, or had a natural dad in our life. The role actually increases because Father God desires so much for His children to reach the totality of what He has for their lives. Jesus related with Father God for connection, not because He didn't know what to do. Connection is to produce power not weakness.

If the father was in the child's life and did not affirm the child in the proper way, it's not too late to have a spiritual father to affirm, regardless of the age. Even if the person has gotten into a homosexual lifestyle. Affirming is never too late.

> *1 Corinthians 4:15a For though ye have ten thousand instructors in Christ, yet have ye not many fathers....*

The spiritual father replenishes, repairs, restores, and renews our thinking to receive our Real Dad, Father God. He is also there as a confidant, counselor, friend, and continued affirmer.

The downside of this fathering business is that many spiritual children do not know how to receive their spiritual father when they enter into their lives. The other side of that coin, the spiritual father, learned how to be a father from whom? There is not a university that you attend to get a degree in fatherhood. I have

> The spiritual father replenishes, repairs, restores, and renews our thinking to receive our Real Dad, Father God.

experienced new spiritual children come into my life, where initially they did not recognize me as spiritual father. I have not kept a record, but on occasion, years pass before they finally receive me as father. There have been other times where I can sense that the new spiritual son/daughter, especially a son, has their defense up, ready and able to defend themselves. The reason: they have been defending themselves all of their lives, never having anyone to fight for them. Scores of times I've had to finally say, "I'm not here to fight you but to love you."

—⸻—

THE DILEMMA OF PILGRIM COMMUNITY CHURCH

Pilgrim Community Church is one of the fastest growing churches in the city. Pastor Jacob is a great teacher and the choir is second to none. Pilgrim was a small struggling church until Pastor J took the helm. Since the first years of his tenure, the church thrived and continues to grow in numbers. But PCC has a dilemma: people come, but the ones looking to connect do not stay long.

Pastor J was so happy when his son revealed that he felt called to the ministry. He attended the finest Bible school. Soon after, as if scripted, he quickly joined his dad in the work of the ministry. But after a few years, the dreaded meeting came. "Dad, I feel the Lord wants me to move to another city."

Pastor J did not grow up with his dad. He loved people. He loved the ministry. Yet he struggled at connecting in real relationships. The main point that The Arbinger Institute brings out in their three books, *The Outward Mindset, Leadership and Self-Deception,* and *The Anatomy of Peace*, is seeing people as people and not as objects. This trilogy of books describe in detail the inward mindset and seeing people as objects instead of people. More times than not when there have not been a training in relationships, it is common practice to focus on our goals or task, and everyone and everything is there to aid us in arriving or completing our task. It's very easy to do. You see it in traffic all the time. It happens in our places of employment. It happened with Pastor J. He didn't have the skills to connect.

This illustration does not depict any real persons past or present. It is from knowledge gained after years of pastoring pastors on a global front.

PASTORS THAT ARE NOT AFFIRMED

The danger of pastors who are not affirmed in their sexuality is that they are natural influencers. That's what they do for a living. There are multiple scriptures instructing the believer to be like, to follow, to imitate your leader.

Some ways and mannerisms are caught, not taught. You become like the ones you hang around. A relationship with a spiritual leader whom you love and respect is unmatched. That's why the leader, pastor, must be aware of any uncleanness operating in and through him/her. I've heard many testimonies of pastor's lives prior to totally submitting to God. The enemy of their soul exhausted all measures to distort their destiny, including on many occasions removing their father from their life. Or at best, causing the dad to be less than valuable. A result of many of those lives is that a homosexual spirit will be prevalent throughout the church they pastor. The sad ending is that no one discusses it; it is whispered about, but never brought to the forefront.

> The absence of father, loving and affirming the child in the way that he/she needs, produces a void.

The absence of a father loving and affirming the child in the way that he/she needs produces a void. Unless that void is filled by a strong mom, coach, uncle, grandpa, or the like, it is so easy for perversion of the person's being and their destiny to occur.

Can you see how a particular environment can change the course of a person? The father is to protect the environment. A true father would not allow his child to be exposed to a harmful environment. There is a forming happening with the people that are consistently around us. We are becoming them. They are becoming us.

Growing up with older parents, they seem to have been more concerned with who our friends were than parents of today. Maybe that's one of the reasons we called them old fashioned.

Environment: the aggregate of surrounding things, conditions, or influences

Environ: to form a circle or ring round.

My circle influences my forming

The one that understands you best is the one that knows and understands your environment. If you don't know my environment, you probably don't know me. That's why emphasis must be placed on your circle. The Father is needed to walk us through our environment, because our environment is to be used to help make us look and act like our father.

Because our environment is used to influence our forming and the father helps in the forming processes, who better to help walk us through the environment than the father natural, spiritual, or Real Father. Father is father.

> Because of the vast lack of knowledge of forming, coupled with the total misunderstanding of the father, there has been an acceptance of homosexuality that was never intended to be accepted.

The things that come into your environment will influence you. As a child of God, you must guard what comes into your environment because your father has a vision for your life. The father wants you to work with him, not against him, so that you may arrive safely to your destiny. Your environment influences your focus; your focus influences your vision/destiny.

Last note on homosexuality

Because the homosexual tendencies are formed in a person, once the same sex behavior is accepted, it is difficult to change. You are formed in that behavior.

Galatians 4:19 My little children, of whom I travail in birth again until Christ be formed in you,

The homosexual situation is a terrible tragedy. Because of the vast lack of knowledge of forming, coupled with the total misunderstanding of the father, there has been an acceptance of homosexuality that was never intended to be accepted.

When discussing homosexuality, there is little discussion of what was the environment of the mother during the forming of the child in the womb. Almost no one speaks of the interaction of the child and the father in reference to forming in their sexuality. These are two key components in the forming of the child, to include their sexuality.

John 10:10 The thief cometh not, but for to steal, and to kill, and to destroy: I am come that they might have life, and that they might have it more abundantly.

LET THE HEALING BEGIN

The following are Healing Questions you may want to ponder alone or with someone you trust.

1. As much as you are able to remember, analyze your environment of the early years of your life. Look at those years in an informative manner, not a judgmental manner.

2. If your dad was in your life, how has his love towards you affected the way you relate to others?

3. If your dad was not in your life, how has his vacancy affected the way you relate to others?

4. Spend quality time praying over the above questions alone or preferably with someone you trust.

5. Have you studied *The Five Love Languages*? Did your dad, or others, use that language to teach you?

6. If your father was in your life as a child, do you feel he used the proper love language in his interactions with you? Discuss how this affected you, good or bad.

7. If you understand learning styles, what is your learning style? Did your dad, or others, use that style to teach you?

8. What if anything, could your dad have done to better afford your affirmation?

9. Spend quality time praying over the above questions alone or preferably with someone you trust.

10. With a view of your sexuality, how would your thinking be categorized toward sexuality? Homosexual or heterosexual? The questions are solely focused on thinking, not actions.

11. As much as you are able to, think about how your forming played a role in your thoughts toward your sexuality.

12. Spend quality time praying over the above questions alone or preferably with someone you trust.

13. If you are currently engaged in a homosexual lifestyle, solicit qualified counseling to help navigate how you arrived at your current lifestyle.

14. If your current thinking is of a homosexual nature, solicit qualified counseling to help navigate how you arrived at your current thinking.

15. Spend quality time praying over all of the above questions alone or preferably with someone you trust.

16. If you understand fasting, add fasting to your prayers. Allow the Holy Spirit to lead you in the task of cleaning the spiritual closet of your past.

CHAPTER FIVE

Dad, TEACH ME HOW TO FIGHT

I WISH I could have interviewed my dad for this book. What was he thinking when he had his sixth son and ninth child at age forty-four? What was he thinking as he interacted with me day after day? Did he think that this time it would be different? Was he thinking about plans to start his own business with me by his side?

Mom and Dad moved to Detroit from Rome, Georgia, somewhere around 1942. I'm sure it was to have a better life for their family. That's the reason Blacks in particular migrated to the North from the Southern States. Dad was a very hard worker, Mom too. Dad held down two to three jobs attempting to make ends meet. Finally around 1956-57 he began working part-time for himself. He cleaned office buildings and cut grass. His persistence paid off with him developing his own lawn care business.

This is the part of the interview where I would sit up on the edge of my seat, lean forward, and ask Dad, "Did you think about where you placed your most emphasis while raising me?"

Dad would say, "WHAT? What are you talking about?"

"Dad, you taught me how to work for money. But, you didn't teach me how to make money work."

No one sat me down and explained anything to me, but I watched Dad leave home and return, day after day. I saw the cupboards, refrigerator, freezer and pantry consistently full. My mental computer recorded Dad driving into the driveway with new vehicles. He was always buying new lawnmowers and other lawn equipment. He never informed me if he paid cash, credit, or if he had a rich uncle hidden somewhere.

Throughout the years, Mom and Dad would load me and my sisters in the car to travel. Were we on vacation? Looking back, it certainly seemed like it. We frequently traveled to my aunts and grandma and grandpa's house in other states. That was so much fun. How'd Dad pay for those trips? We're talking early 60s, a black family traveling to and fro on the highways. Was dad really that fearless? Oh how I wish I could've interviewed Dad.

Dad was a stout, muscular, very handsome mulatto man. Dad always appeared well dressed even in his starched work uniforms. His Sunday go-to-meeting white shirts had so much starch in them, they could stand up on the floor like a mannequin. Dad gave an appearance to his fragile and youngest son that he could do anything but fail.

Since I didn't get to interview Dad for this book (he died in 1988), I surmise that his love language was gifts. For years dad didn't give me a salary, he bought me unsolicited gifts. If I could have interviewed him, I would have asked, what took so long for him to start paying me. He paid his other employees. Why did he fight me and Mom for so long about a paycheck? He behaved like we were business partners. My share was room and board. There was an occasional fringe benefit but not a consistent paycheck. Why Dad?

Once upon a time, Mom was gone for days, without the interview I don't know where she went. Dad and my sisters remodeled the living and dining room, complete with new

> Fathers, do not provoke your children, lest they become discouraged. Colossians 3:21

furniture. I remember Mom being so happy and pleased upon her return. How'd Dad pay for that? There was a consistent flow (maybe flow is a strong word) of appliances, house paintings, new landscaping, and the like. How'd Dad pay for all that stuff? Dad wasn't rich. I think my mental computer thought that he was. He wasn't.

I didn't know this back in the day, but Mom and Dad had three sets of children. My five brothers, my three sisters, and me. This is why I label us three sets. The older boys were born in Rome. Who knows what these guys experienced? After all, it was the 20s, 30s, and 40s in Georgia. Dad could be a little harsh. Dad had a very strong loud voice. Dad could be blunt. Okay, Dad could appear like a very mean guy. Dad provoked his children to anger, contrary to Scripture.

Fathers, do not provoke your children, lest they become discouraged. Colossians 3:21

I'm not sure if Dad ever read that Scripture. In fact, I'm sure Dad never read that Scripture. So, my brothers did not experience the "regenerated dad," after he had given his life to Christ. They never knew the "business owner dad" to the degree that I experienced him. My sisters knew the "hard working dad." They knew the, "give dad his proper respect, dad."

They knew the, "he's the guy that provides for us, dad." They saw the relaxed jovial dad when we traveled or when we had company. But those were on rare occasions. Then there was yours truly. The baby. I was treated somewhat different. Three sisters, one boy, "Yeah, he's different." My sisters would sometimes say, "Dad's always buying you something." (Actually, just one sister in particular.) "Hey, give me a break, I'm the one going to work with him everyday." I should have said.

I'm not trying to paint a bad dad here. Give the guy a break, he had nine children. My quest is to take you back to reveal how a dad can demonstrate God to his child without knowing that's what he's doing.

Now that you've come this far in *The Dad Book*, read Psalm 23 with a different set of eyes. Stand behind David's great-grandfather Boaz, his grandfather Obed, and his father Jesse. Now read the passage with the knowledge that the teachings, trainings, security, and wealth of these fathers have been impressed into David.

There was a relative of Naomi's husband, a man of great wealth, of the family of Elimelech. His name was Boaz. Ruth 2:1

And they called his name Obed. He is the father of Jesse, the father of David. Ruth 4:17b

Psalm 23:1 The LORD is my shepherd; I shall not want. 2 He maketh me to lie down in green pastures: he leadeth me beside the still waters. 3 He restoreth my soul: he leadeth me in the paths of righteousness for his name's sake. 4 Yea, though I walk through the valley of the shadow of death, I will fear no evil: for thou art with me; thy rod and thy staff they comfort me. 5 Thou preparest a table before me in the presence of mine enemies: thou anointest my head with oil; my cup runneth over. 6 Surely goodness and mercy shall follow me all the days of my life: and I will dwell in the house of the LORD for ever.

You can clearly see how David was able to receive his REAL DAD, Father God with ease. The road had been paved. It was a natural transition

> A father affirms - builds confidence- trains thinking

with all the awesome dads standing behind him. You can also see, how much one has lost, when they are not afforded that long line of dads.

So David, the shepherd boy, was not just any young lad watching over his father's sheep. He was a lad that was secure in who he was. The boy had the confidence to ward off a lion and a bear! How about the Goliath encounter? Can you see how he had the courage to behave as he did? David had the security of the father his entire life. He could do all things because he had been strengthened by his dads.

Philippians 4:13 I can do all things through Christ who strengthens me.

The reason we do not see more followers of Christ operating in the above Scripture is because they have no frame of reference.

A father affirms - builds confidence- trains thinking

Once upon a time, long, long ago on Father's Day, I was a visiting preacher at an inner city church. I preached what I thought was a pretty good message. From the response of the audience, they didn't agree. I preached about a powerful, loving Father who loved unconditionally. I told of His forgiving nature and unmerited grace. No response. What? After my customary pleasantries, I went home and whined to God. Excuse me, I meant to say, prayed to God. After my emotions were expressed, I could clearly hear Him say, "No frame of reference."

Now I could see the congregation as He saw them. Hurt and fragmented, displaced in life by the absence of the one that impregnated their mother.

—❭❙❬—

MARTINEZ WAS HER NAME

Once while returning home from a ministry time, my wife and I
looked at a menu while waiting for our server at a restaurant in
the airport. I had no idea I was about to meet a server I would be
talking about for years to come. Every person I meet is like a book
in my imaginary library. I only have a short encounter with most
of those books. I try to maximize
the time by quickly perusing the
book as fast as I can. To do so, I
ask a lot of questions. I try to get
them to smile and open up to me

> "I didn't grow up with my
> dad." THAT'S how she
> responded.

in any way that I can get them to do so. Some books are harder
to read than others. They teach me so much as they enter my perpetual virtual library. Today was no different. Our server looked
Spanish; her name tag said she was Spanish. I could not imagine what weight her small stature was carrying. "Señorita, buenos
días." I beamed. She replied, "I didn't grow up with my dad."
THAT'S how she responded.

My new book that had just fallen off the library shelf of life into the
lap of my mind was one of the most intriguing books I had ever encountered. Her Spanish last name on her name tag was not a name
tag at all. That tag meant so much more to her than just a name. It
was more of a tag than a name tag. By the way it was a last name,
not a first name. Every waiter or waitress that I've ever run into
always has a first name on their name tag. This was a first for me.

To her that tag said,

All I have from my father is his name.

I don't have a relationship with my dad.

I don't know who I am, but this is my father's name.

Do you know my father?

Do you have the same last name as me?

Could you possibly know my dad?

As many people that come into this restaurant, there is a possibility that my dad or someone who knows him could enter this place.

I understand how Jesus must have felt looking at His people. He was sent to what He called the lost sheep of Israel. Without the security of the father, one can appear like Martinez. Lost.

Matthew 9:36 But when He saw the multitudes, He was moved with compassion for them, because they were weary and scattered, like sheep having no shepherd.

The security that a dad brings into the life of the child is immeasurable

Jesse was indirectly showing David the security of the father when he sent David to check on his brothers. Even though they were in a war, the father wanted to know how his boys were doing. The father builds security into the child by letting the child know that the father is always there. But, you can also see that there is a noticeable difference in the relationship of David and his dad versus Jesse and his other sons. A similar expression is shown with Jacob and his son Joseph.

> The security that a dad brings into the life of the child is immeasurable

1 Samuel 17:17–18 Then Jesse said to his son David, "Take now for your brothers an ephah of this dried grain and these ten loaves, and run to your brothers at the camp. 18 And carry these ten cheeses to the captain of their thousand, and see how your brothers fare, and bring back news of them."

Genesis 37:3–4 Now Israel loved Joseph more than all his children, because he was the son of his old age. Also he made him a tunic of many colors. 4 But when his brothers saw that their father loved him more than all his brothers, they hated him and could not speak peaceably to him.

The natural dad as well as the spiritual dad, as they grow in age, may have a tendency to interact with their sons and daughters according to their destiny. Father God does the same but it is not as evident.

Jesse sent David to check on his brothers, but he was also positioning him for the stage of life that would lead him into his destiny. Jacob (Israel) loved Joseph in a way that not only caused him to receive love, but it showed him how to love.

Being the youngest of nine children, afforded me the life of love by all my brothers and sisters along with my dad and mom. I heard stories of my brothers arguing over who would hold me and rock me to sleep. My family placed love in the fiber of my being. I now have the ability to love in a way that surprises me sometimes. I am now able to love entire cities and nations. That's my call. Thanks family.

> Some of these blessed sons and daughters are so secure in who they are, they have a tendency to step out from under that security too soon.

But, there is another side of this security thing; I've experienced that side too.

THE DOWNSIDE OF THE SECURITY OF THE FATHER

When a son or daughter has never experienced life *without* the security of the father, they may find themselves taking that security for granted. Some of these blessed sons and daughters are so secure in who they are, they have a tendency to step out from under that security too soon. Or, they may be so secure in who they are, they may venture into something without giving the consequences much thought. These attitudes can prove dangerous.

> *2 Samuel 11:2–4 Then it happened one evening that David arose from his bed and walked on the roof of the king's house. And from the roof he saw a woman bathing, and the woman was very beautiful to behold. 3 So David sent and inquired about the woman. And someone said, "Is this not Bathsheba, the daughter of Eliam, the wife of Uriah the Hittite?" 4 Then David sent messengers, and took her; and she came to him, and he lay with her, for she was cleansed from her impurity; and she returned to her house.*

How could David do such a vile thing? Certainly he knew better. This was the same David that was known as a wise man. This was the same David that we had all come to know and love.

Let me show you another David.

> *Luke 15:11–13 Then He said: "A certain man had two sons. 12 And the younger of them said to his father, 'Father, give me the portion of goods that falls to me.' So he divided to them his livelihood. 13 And not many days after, the younger son gathered all together, journeyed to a far country, and there wasted his possessions with prodigal living.*

His name may or may not have been David, but he behaved just as dumb as David. You know this young man's end. He wasted his father's inheritance and found himself so low he was lusting after the pig's food.

Both of these Davids returned to the father. They had different circumstances, but they both had the security of the father. We know David's history of dads: it's clearly written in Scripture and we have discussed it here. The other prodigal David, we don't know as much about his lineage. However, there is enough substantial evidence to conclude they both behaved as one that had their father in their life. Yes, both of their actions were wrong. No, everyone that has their dad in their life does not behave as these two. But both behaved confidently. They saw something they wanted and went after it. Were they right in their actions? We all know the answer to that. But most successful people speak freely of the education gained in their failures.

Both Davids (Forgive me for calling the prodigal son David. But you must admit David sounds better than what most people call him) came back to the father.

Luke 15:17–19 "But when he came to himself, he said, 'How many of my father's hired servants have bread enough and to spare, and I perish with hunger! 18 I will arise and go to my father, and will say to him, "Father, I have sinned against heaven and before you, 19 and I am no longer worthy to be called your son. Make me like one of your hired servants." '

With King David we see a clearer picture of remorse displayed that's easy to relate to. David had been released to his Real Dad after being privy to a strong father lineage. He had lost something with Father God as a result of his sin that shook his very existence. Sin cut him off from his relationship with Father God. We see that with David II too, but his is a natural severing; David's is a spiritual one.

Psalm 51 is David's heart poured out in repentance of his foolish actions and consequences of his separation from Father God.

> *Psalm 51:10–13 Create in me a clean heart, O God, And renew a steadfast spirit within me. 11 Do not cast me away from Your presence, And do not take Your Holy Spirit from me. 12 Restore to me the joy of Your salvation, And uphold me by Your generous Spirit. 13 Then I will teach transgressors Your ways, And sinners shall be converted to You.*

David said in essence, I don't ever want to lose what I had with You! Nothing is worth being separated from Your presence. David II's confession was similar,

> *Luke 15:20–21 And he arose, and came to his father. But when he was yet a great way off, his father saw him, and had compassion, and ran, and fell on his neck, and kissed him. 21 And the son said unto him, Father, I have sinned against heaven, and in thy sight, and am no more worthy to be called thy son.*

They were both like, "This is crazy. What am I doing? As good as the security of the father is and I'm out here behaving like this?"

Psalm 51 is David's heart poured out in repentance of his foolish actions and consequences of his separation from Father God.

Again, I am not condoning their actions. Their actions aren't as important. It's their response to their behavior that shows they have the security of the father. They were confident, right or wrong. In your confidence there is a responsibility, which we'll discuss later. The wealth gained by having the security of dad in your life is immeasurable. And, it must not be taken for granted.

SPIRITUAL FATHERS GIVE SECURITY TOO

The security of the father does not end with the natural father and Father God. Being a spiritual father, I know for certain that you cannot fulfill the vision in your heart without spiritual children. Spiritual children cannot fulfill their vision without spiritual fathers. God created us to live, work, and play within families.

> *1 Timothy 1:18 This charge I commit to you, son Timothy, according to the prophecies previously made concerning you, that by them you may wage the good warfare,*

> *1 Corinthians 4:16–17 Therefore I urge you, imitate me. 17 For this reason I have sent Timothy to you, who is my beloved and faithful son in the Lord, who will remind you of my ways in Christ, as I teach everywhere in every church.*

Son does not denote child or sub but relationship. Spiritual father does not denote all-knowing or boss but the same as natural father. Some may say they do not need a spiritual father either because of ignorance or because they have seen abusive fathers in the faith.

> *Hebrews 13:17 Obey them that have the rule over you, and submit yourselves: for they watch for your souls, as they that must give account, that they may do it with joy, and not with grief: for that is unprofitable for you.*

"Watch for your souls." When Jesse sent David to check on his brothers, he was watching for their souls. Your soul is your mind, thought processes. Your soul is your emotions. Your soul is the choices you make. Life as well as ministry goes a lot smoother when you have a father in your life watching for your soul.

A spiritual father is not in your life to control but to enhance and give security. You know you have someone on the planet that has your back, someone that doesn't want anything from you. The only thing desired is for you to be successful. That's a spiritual father.

Are there those that say they are spiritual fathers who do not understand that? You bet. There are those in the natural that think they can be a father but have no idea what a father is. There are those that even think they are god, because they do not fear or know the true God.

> Life as well as ministry, goes a lot smoother when you have a father in your life watching for your soul.

Regardless of how many wrongs there are, they do not eliminate the right. However, it may cause the right to be harder to locate.

In other words, regardless of how many horror stories of improper fathering, we still need a father. The problem the improper fathering perpetuates, is to make it harder to receive from a true father. Especially Father God.

LET THE HEALING BEGIN

The following are Healing Questions you may want to ponder alone or with someone you trust.

In these healing questions, the security of the Father term will be used whether dad was there or not.

1. Look at your life. Has the security of the father been there? Discuss that in depth.

2. How has your life been hampered or helped as result of the security of the father?

3. Is there any unforgiveness as a result of the security of the father?

4. Is there a need for repentance as a result of the security of the father?

5. If you had the security of the father, have you noticed the downside? Are there areas in your life where you need help as a result of the downside?

6. Do you find it difficult, or not, to receive a spiritual father? Why?

7. In your opinion, do you feel you or anyone, for that matter, needs a spiritual father? Why?

8. Do you have a spiritual father in your life currently? Does it help, hinder or neither?

9. How do you feel regarding the phrase, "Watch for your souls?"

10. Have you been hurt by a spiritual father? If so, have you completely come to terms with the circumstance?

CHAPTER SIX

The VOICE OF THE FATHER

"God is God. Because he is God, He is worthy of my trust and obedience. I will find rest nowhere but in His holy will that is unspeakably beyond my largest notions of what he is up to."

— Elisabeth Elliot

The problem I have with my daughter Melanie is that she'd rather call on the phone than text. She says she wants to know the tone of the words, not just the words alone. She wants to hear what you're saying, not read it. Thanks Melanie.

Growing up, my dad's voice was a major force in my life. "DAVID!!!"

Let me describe it this way, those times of hearing urgency in his voice from a distance immediately invoked fear. Dad was what some would call a "man's man." Compare this big heavyset man of a man with a loud strong voice to an overprotected eight to thirteen-year-old boy. My beginning years were spent with Mom and my sisters, while Dad was gone all day working. We've mentioned how Dad started a small business and I was his first employee. And I've told you, the word employee is really stretching it.

So, at the ripe old age of eight years old, Dad and I started a weekly routine. We spent time together every day after school and all day in the summer. I quickly learned that Dad's bark was worse than his bite. Having this insight into Dad's behavioral patterns didn't relieve me of my fear of hearing that loud voice calling my name. Sometimes I knew what he wanted, other times I was stunned, and wondered, "What'd I do this time?" One thing is for sure, I never hollered back: "Leave me alone Dad, call someone else. I'm busy."

A father affirms - builds confidence- trains thinking

My training with Dad's voice started after I had been trained by Mom's voice. This was reinforced by my sisters' voices. They were kinder and gentler. My life quickly transitioned from "my baby boy" and "my little brother" to, "BOY! DID YOU HEAR ME, BOY?" I thought my name had been changed to Boy. "Yes sir." Was I in for a big change in lifestyle.

Understanding the parallel of the three fathers that God desires in the life of His children: biological, Father God, and spiritual father, brings clarity to the necessity of father in one's life. It also invokes healing to those who have been hurt by a father.

Colossians 3:21 Fathers, provoke not your children to anger, lest they be discouraged.

Ephesians 6:4 And, ye fathers, provoke not your children to wrath: but bring them up in the nurture and admonition of the Lord.

I've used these scriptures a lot because the father has to live by them! The way the natural and/or spiritual father relates with the offspring is a

> A father affirms - builds confidence- trains thinking

psychological programming of how one relates with Father God.

What happens to children who do not receive instructions from their biological father on obeying the voice of the father? The results of this tragedy are endless. I believe the biggest tragedy is the disrespect and disobedience to all male authority. At its worst, disobeying all authority regardless of gender is disheartening.

The line of demarcation is drawn between the relationship of father and offspring. To change a person, you begin with thinking. Father teaches thinking, hence, remove father, and conquering thinking becomes easier for the enemy of our souls. This father thing is really simple; we make it difficult. That's why I have repeated some things often.

Allow me to use the illustration of the two sides to the father/child coin again. On one hand, the father fights to be the best father for the child. Flip it. The child fights to receive the love from the father that's so desperately needed. Both are fought to stop that destiny. The father's attack may have started before he was born. So it traveled down through his lineage until he had his first child. The child may not even know that he/she needs the love of the father. So it comes out in other ways, causing him/her to be labeled this, that, or the other thing. All the child wanted is the love of the father.

In a male it may come out as aggression, anger, or violence. With a female it may surface as promiscuity. The male is void of leadership training. The female is void of proper love shown by father minus the sexual intimacy.

On several occasions while serving in the capacity as pastor, I've been prompted by the Holy Spirit to share with someone that was in need of emotional healing from the loss of a father, "He has no idea what he never had." The offspring is such an awesome person, yet their father never experienced their awesomeness. Likewise the person in need of healing has a hole in their heart for the missing father.

⚊⟍⎮⫽⚊

BIG JOHN LITTLE JOHN

John Cartwright wasn't called Big John until he had a son. He had told himself, when I have a son I'm naming him after me. So he did. Big John met Mercy in high school. The two immediately fell in love. Their relationship quickly moved from a kiss goodbye to having sex several times a week. John never met his dad, he went to prison soon after John was born. There was never any contact between his mom and his dad. His name or any mention of him was rarely brought up. Mercy's family was somewhat similar. Her mom dated a married man from her job, who became Mercy's dad after a drunken and heavy drug indulging party. Neither one wanted a baby, the man, because he was married; Mercy's mom, because she wasn't married. But as Mercy's mom realized day after day that she was carrying a little person inside of her, she embraced her circumstance and wanted to keep her baby. Mercy was born. Mercy's mom and her dad never spoke again. All communications between them ceased. Mercy's mom birthed her and raised her all alone. Growing up, John and Mercy each knew something was missing in their lives but had no idea what that something was.

After years of life's grind, Big John, Mercy, and Little John grew apart from one another. Big John worked shift work at the nearby power plant. Mercy taught fifth graders at Carver Middle School.

Little John, aka LJ, was buried in every sport on the planet. He seem to excel in them all. Soon Mercy begin to have an unusual amount of meetings after school. Mercy was not at meetings, though that's what she told her family mostly on the sticky notes stuck on the aluminum foil covering their dinner in the fridge.

How is Mercy going to tell Big John she's pregnant? How is she not going to tell him that the baby is Coach Don's baby. After preparing a Sunday meal fit for a king, Mercy slips into the gown that Big John bought her for Valentine's Day the year before. He loves that gown. Just as Big John's mouth is watering for the Sunday's dessert he's about to receive, she spills it.

"John I'm pregnant." Big John's words caught Mercy off guard. "How?" John says. "How, we haven't had sex since Moses brought the children of Israel out of Egypt!"

Mercy remained calm while reminding her husband of the time it probably happened. Mercy went to bed that night unsure if Big John was convinced that Coach Don's baby growing inside of her was his.

Big John hated the baby, and the fact that he didn't look like him was not the reason. He just didn't connect with the boy. The baby grew into a boy. A big boy. A really big boy. LJ loved having a brother. They were inseparable.

Then it happened. Carver Middle School's football team won the championship. Guess who was on the news being interviewed how he produced the winningest middle school football team in the district? Coach Don. The Coach Don that looks exactly like Big John's son! The Coach Don that works at the same school as

Big John's wife. The Coach Don that is probably Big John's son's daddy!

Big John never discussed his discovery with Mercy or his son that wasn't his son, aka Don Jr. From that day forward Big John treated Luke, aka Don, Jr like Cinderella, and he was the mean mother. He had nothing but harsh words for Luke.

A few weeks after the *60 Minutes* discovery, Easter rolled around. All the families were taking family portraits. Next it was the Cartwright's turn. Mercy beckoned for the two boys Little John and Luke to "Come on, it's time to take our pictures." Big John harshly hollered at Luke, "NOT YOU! GET ON AWAY FROM HERE!"

Luke was devastated. He was devastated two times. Mom didn't defend him. LJ said nothing too. He went on the side of the church building and cried the front of his freshly ironed yellow shirt wet as if water had been spilt on it.

Luke's life changed that day. It changed again a few years later when he discovered why.

(The story and characters have been created from years of counseling and do not represent any individuals past or present.)

John 10:1-5 "Most assuredly, I say to you, he who does not enter the sheepfold by the door, but climbs up some other way, the same is a thief and a robber. 2 But he who enters by the door is the shepherd of the sheep. 3 To him the doorkeeper opens, and the sheep hear his voice; and he calls his own sheep by name and leads them out. 4 And when he brings out his own sheep, he goes before them; and the sheep follow him, for they know his voice. 5 Yet they will by no means follow a stranger, but will flee from him, for they do not know the voice of strangers."

> Humans respond in a similar manner as sheep. Man is made to submit to a higher authority.

In this passage, Jesus is aptly describing the traits of the relationship that sheep have with their shepherd. It's directly associated with his voice. The sheep must be watched over during the night because of thieves. When the shepherd returns the next morning, they leave with the shepherd, simply following his voice.

Matthew 9:36 But when He saw the multitudes, He was moved with compassion for them, because they were weary and scattered, like sheep having no shepherd.

In our modern world, we may be hard pressed to find a flock of sheep. I've heard and read of the beauty of the large or small herd of sheep following behind their leader. To see such a sight makes it easier to understand why Jesus used the sheep illustration to teach the disciples about hearing and obeying. In some instances I understand shepherds even have names for their sheep. They have a connection with the voice of their shepherd, and all other voices are foreign to them, even inflicting fear when heard.

Humans respond in a similar manner as sheep. Man is made to submit to a higher authority. In our daily actions, we are searching for the thing to do, right or wrong. We don't know what to eat, yet we're hungry and the refrigerator is full! We don't know what to wear, but we're late for our appointment. It doesn't matter that the closet is full, even sprinkled with new outfits! We are made to submit, to ask, to seek, to look outward.

Good leaders know that when you have decisions to make, you go with your gut. It's an unspoken voice that says, pick that one, do this or do that. The more comfortable you become with this process, the more your choices are confirmed. The better you become at making decisions. You don't second guess your decision. You go with it. That's what Dad teaches.

One of the main tasks of a father is to teach decision making. As father is teaching this course, you're learning his voice. Fathers are wired to teach. If life's experiences have to teach decision making, it can prove to be quite grueling. And this is another area spiritual fathers are truly helpful.

LIFE'S TEACHINGS CAN BE DISASTROUS

Once upon a time, I watched a movie about a couple that wanted to go on a tour of the Grand Canyon for their honeymoon. I'll convey the short version because I don't recall the name of the movie or the characters' names. Upon arrival at the Grand Canyon they were told by the authorities, "I'm sorry, but you need a guide with the proper papers to enter. The office that authorizes permits into the Canyon is closed for the weekend. Besides, there aren't any more guides. You'll have to come back on Monday." They were devastated.

A similar scenario happens in the lives of people every day. THEY NEED TO HEAR A VOICE.

In this case, they were set up to hear a voice that would lead to their demise. A conman guide overheard their predicament and told the couple that he had the proper papers to take them into the Grand Canyon. They followed this shyster into the abyss, not knowing that death for two of them was close behind. One must learn to not listen and follow every voice heard but to know the father's voice distinctly.

DISOBEDIENCE NEVER PAYS OFF

Years ago, I was in the retail store with my two-year-old child. The love of shopping entered into her life at about that age and has grown with no signs of diminishing. I was sure she was as interested as her father searching for whatever drove us to that department store. My scrutinizing manner soon bored my little companion, and unbeknownst, to me she was off on her own quest. When I noticed she was not in sight, I frantically began to search for her. The large store must have seemed like a maze against her small stature. Thank God she had the sense to go to the Customer Service desk to ask someone to please find her dad.

Of course, her mother and I told my little companion on several occasions to stay close. Let me jump sides and quickly become this little person's defense attorney. She had been shopping several times in her short span on the planet. She'd traveled more in her brief time on earth than many in a lifetime. She had become experienced at going into the world and safely coming home in one piece. After all, she'd traveled to many places in her short life.

Many have been told to stay close, stay on the path. Many know what is right and what is terribly wrong. Like my little companion, they've done the same thing, time and time again receiving the same outcomes. Yet, they disobey the voice and end up at the customer service desk of life.

"Please help me find my dad."

THE TV IS A POOL OF VOICES

It is irritating to see scores of TV commercials interrupting your life and attempting to sell you something that is the best thing since sliced bread.

"And it is only $19.95 to the first 100 callers. And this deal is not going to last long." "Call right now." "Pick up the phone and dial area code 222-555-5555, NOW!" As soon as that one is finished, another one blares

> There is something innate in a father that causes him to teach, train and instruct the offspring to do exactly as told.

that you can lose 30 pounds in two weeks all the while eating anything you like. Still another commercial comes on selling you a vehicle, and they tell you the cost by informing you how low the monthly payments are. "And this brand new XYZ is only $349.99 per month."

"Well, golly gee. Why don't we rush right down and buy two of those, Ma? We can get two for only $700. a month. Come on, get your coat. Let's go."

We hear voices all day, all of our lives, inside of our minds and all around us. Which one do we adhere to?

And when he brings out his own sheep, he goes before them; and the sheep follow him, for they know his voice. (John 10:4)

There is something innate in a father that causes him to teach, train, and instruct the offspring to do exactly as told. When a task is done incorrectly, it's followed with demonstration of the proper method. If instructions are carried out suitably, there's a show of pleasure.

This is the place where you holler at the book, "You don't know my dad, he's not like that." or "Are you kidding? I could never do anything right in the eyes of THAT man." Stay focused; keep referring to the biblical definition of father,

A father affirms - builds confidence- trains thinking.

—\|/—

LINDA DISCOVERS HIS VOICE

Growing up, Linda's dad was never around. The only voice she heard was Mom or Grandma. Mom seemed to always holler and Linda grew accustomed to the loud sound that meant Mom was displeased but soon she'd get over it. Linda's mom worked a full-time job and a part-time one to provide for Linda and her sister. Linda didn't have a clue that Mom was financially strapped. After all, she and her little sister seemed to always get what they wanted. Mom didn't have a lot of time to spend with her girls, but when she did they had loads of fun. One time, Linda was so happy Mom was teaching her how to make her favorite- sweet potato pie. According to Linda, there was nothing on earth that tasted better than Momma's homemade pies.

> A father affirms - builds confidence- trains thinking.

The thirteen-year-old watched intently as Mom took her step by step through the process. Her mind had become a camera, a recording device, and a search engine all in one as Momma's kitchen turned into Linda's laboratory. Then it was time to put the pie in the oven. "Let me do it Momma, let me do it, please," said Linda. "Okay, slowly now, be careful, take your time," Momma said. (This is the place in the story where heaven ends and hell begins.) For many years after that day, Linda asked herself, "Why did the doorbell have to ring at that exact moment?"

"Oh my God, Lin-DA, I can't believe you dropped MY PIE GIRL!" Momma fussed and hollered for what seemed like the next two hours. Linda was not on punishment. She was not banished to her room. She was not banned from TV, phone, or extracurricular activities. But she had to listen to Mom's voice about dropping pies until Jesus returned.

Time led Linda on a path of physical and mental struggles: the birth of a son, a failed marriage, and financial hardship. It was a natural progression for Linda to find herself in church one day because a friend asked her to go. After all, a laundry room full of dirty clothes, her usual companion on Sunday, would wait until she returned home.

That Sunday morning was the beginning for Linda. Sitting in church that wintry sunny day, with most congregants wrapped in their winter coats and scarves, seemed to Linda as if she was watching a movie. She was sitting next to her friend who knew everything about her but her social security number. She heard the preacher say something about the voice of the Father. She left the room, but her body remained next to her friend.

"The voice of the father?" thought Linda. "I don't remember my dad's voice." she exclaimed within herself. Linda's thought pattern from that point on was as if she were dumbfounded with her mouth wide open. At that point Linda's friend glanced over at her. Linda had a blank stare on her face. Her eyes were glaring at the preacher. "Boy, she's really into his sermon. Frankly, it's a little boring this morning, but thank God she's enjoying it," her friend thought.

When Linda's mind returned from its travels through her life, she found herself weeping uncontrollably at the altar of the church sanctuary. She was kind of embarrassed and lightheaded as she looked around at her fellow penitents.

There wasn't much conversation riding home. Linda stared out the window of the passenger seat window watching the sun dance off of the mounds of week old snow on the ground. "What just happened?" she interrogated herself.

Linda began a quest of devouring the Bible as if it were a romantic, action-packed, bestselling novel. Something new was happening to her. She'd never been here before. She had gone to Sunday school on occasion growing up. Mom worked many Sundays, but when they spent Saturday night at Grandma's house, she always rose early for church the next morning and always called out, "C'mon now, girls. Get up, I can't miss church now."

> Of the seven and one half billion people in the world, how many have never heard their father's voice?

Linda had bought a Bible many years ago. After all, it seemed right to have a Bible in the house. Until now, the pages had not been introduced to light. A beginning was happening as the new student pulled the Bible off her bedroom night stand and snuggled up with her new friend.

Of the seven-and-one-half-billion people in the world, how many have never heard their father's voice? Just the mere thought is staggering. How many Lindas are there in that seven billion?

(The story and characters have been created from years of counseling and do not represent any individuals present or past.)

Knowing and obeying the father's voice is a good start. The ultimate is prompt obedience.

Have you ever noticed that many of the great men of the Bible were shepherds? Abraham, Isaac, Jacob, Moses, David. As national leaders, both Moses and David were shepherds over Israel.

PROMPT OBEDIENCE

Learn to move when the father tells you to move or you may miss what you are to receive at the next destination.

In 1 Samuel 17:17-20, Jesse was very specific in his instructions to his son. Dad told son, to take 50 pounds of corn, and ten loves of bread to his brothers. To the captain, take ten cheeses, it was probably a large amount of cheese because dad said give it to the captain over a thousand, not fifty or a hundred. Smart move Jesse. David was instructed to check on his brothers, see if they needed anything, and report back to him. This was an important assignment, with a large cargo. What did David do? He rose early and departed to do exactly what he was instructed.

Because of prompt obedience, what Jesse, David's dad, told him to do became primary. What David was doing when Jesse gave him the instructions became secondary. You may or may not want to stop doing what you're doing when the father tells you to do a different task. That is not in the equation. When you have learned prompt obedience of the father, you're ready for promotion. Natural dad is to teach you prompt obedience so that when you receive your Real Dad, Father God, the rewards of prompt obedience is life changing. God loves obedience. He loves prompt obedience even more.

You know the account of David and Goliath. From obeying his dad, David entered onto the scene of life that changed the course of the nation of Israel.

You don't obey the father according to the destination; you obey regardless of the destination.

The father may send you into the battle that will propel you into your destiny.

The father may send you to a place that will be used to bring you to the forefront.

Suppose David had told his father that he didn't want to go to the battlefield?

There is a relationship that the son and daughter have with the voice of the father that is unparalleled.

The voice of the father has with it authority that is not associated with any other person.

I love the story of the Centurion in Luke Chapter Seven. He understood like no other that the voice of Jesus was under Jesus' authority. That understanding excited Jesus so much because His whole teaching was all

> The voice of the father has with it authority that is not associated with any other person.

about the authority of the voice of the Father. That is what the believer is all about: understanding the voice of the Father, obeying the voice of the Father. Then, using the voice of the Father by wielding His word in Scripture.

The Father spoke the world into existence and speaks to his son/daughter the same way. The way a father speaks to his child can either turn them away or cause them to follow him forever. One of the main goals of the father is to teach the child to speak with authority.

Father: One who actuates (to incite to action) and governs their minds

Abraham takes the cake when it comes to prompt obedience!

There is not much in the Bible of the relationship of Abraham and his dad, Terah. Scripture tells us his dad was a priest and that he worshipped a false god. However, we see Abraham exuding prompt obedience. Whether he learned that trait from his father or elsewhere, it is something that a father teaches his child. Let's give father Terah the credit since no one can dispute it.

> Father: One who actuates (to incite to action) and governs their minds

> *Genesis 22:2-3 And he said, Take now thy son, thine only son Isaac, whom thou lovest, and get thee into the land of Moriah; and offer him there for a burnt offering upon one of the mountains which I will tell thee of. 3 And Abraham rose up early in the morning, and saddled his ass, and took two of his young men with him, and Isaac his son, and clave the wood for the burnt offering, and rose up, and went unto the place of which God had told him.*

Abraham's prompt obedience to God is the ultimate test of obeying the voice of the Father.

Let's zoom in on this day in the life of Abraham. Isaac was not one of many sons, affording Abraham a choice. If that were the case, he may have dubbed the one that gave him the most trouble. No, this was his only son. Remember, he had sent Ishmael away; this was the son that he loved. This was his heir the seed God had promised him! Ought we all to walk in that level of obeying the voice of the Father?

Mount Moriah is the place God told Abraham to take Isaac for the sacrifice. Understanding the Hebrew definition of that word adds light to the path of obeying the voice of the father. The father has a reason for testing our level of obedience. Prompt obedience is the highway to a successful destiny.

Moriah = "chosen by Jehovah"

The Father has chosen a place for your release, but if you do not learn to obey His voice, you will miss your release, elevation, and destiny.

Genesis 22:11 And the angel of the LORD called unto him out of heaven, and said, Abraham, Abraham: and he said, Here am I. 12 And he said, Lay not thine hand upon the lad, neither do thou any thing unto him: for now I know that thou fearest God, seeing thou hast not withheld thy son, thine only son from me. 13 And Abraham lifted up his eyes, and looked, and behold behind him a ram caught in a thicket by his horns: and Abraham went and took the ram, and offered him up for a burnt offering in the stead of his son.

> The father speaks over your life "now I know" by watching how you obey his voice.

Abraham would not have heard God say, "Now I know" had he not obeyed His voice to take his only son and sacrifice him.

The father speaks over your life "now I know" by watching how you obey his voice.

When one fails to look at life as a path, journey, or destination, you may do anything your feelings or thought process suggests. It's likened to someone left to wander in the wilderness of life on a never-ending path to nowhere.

Walking with Father God, biological father, or spiritual father in life is to be a training process to the release into your destiny. Learning to obey the voice of the father is a major part of that process.

LET THE HEALING BEGIN

Meditate and/or pray alone or with someone you trust over the following 10 points on obeying the father's voice.

- Know the Father's voice distinctly.

- Do not listen and follow every voice that you hear.

- Prompt obedience! Learn (or continue) to move when the Father tells you to move. You do not want to miss the reason you were sent.

- The destination the Father is sending you to, does not dictate whether you obey or not. You obey his voice regardless of where He sends you.

- The voice of the father has with it an authority that is not associated with any other voice.

- The way a father speaks to his child can either turn them away or cause them to follow him forever.

- One of the attributes of having a father is that he indirectly teaches you to speak with authority.

- God has chosen a place for your release, but if you do not learn to obey His voice you may miss your elevation and release into your destiny.

- The Father speaks over your life "Now I know" by watching how you obey His voice.

- You will not reach the apex of life without understanding and practicing obedience to the voice of the Father.

"Does it make sense to pray for guidance about the future if we are not obeying in the thing that lies before us today? How many momentous events in Scripture depended on one person's seemingly small act of obedience! Rest assured: Do what God tells you to do now, and, depend upon it, you will be shown what to do next."

— Elisabeth Elliot, *Quest for Love: True Stories of Passion and Purity*

CHAPTER SEVEN

Your RESPONSIBILITY BEGINS: BREAKING THE CYCLE

RESPONSIBILITY: THE QUALITY or condition of being responsible; obligation to a person or thing for which one is responsible.

What would be the responsibility of having a father? First, what did it cost the dad to get you to be where you are? If your dad is not in your life, why not? What was the cost for him to be taken from you? What was given in exchange for what you lost? That may sound like a confused question, but it is not. Someone paid a price for you to have lack. Was it crime? Death? Careless living? Those are prices. So when you punch that up in the responsibility column, what part do you play?

Let's say my dad went to jail for something he did when I was a child. Let's say he was in jail all my life. He missed me growing up: all of my birthdays, ball games, recitals, church picnics, the works. I never knew he tried to get in touch with me because my mom kept him away. She feared I'd turn out like him.

Then I discovered the truth. He didn't grow up with his dad either. He got his education in the hard knocks of the streets. His mother had five other children, all by different dads. When I finally met him, I discovered that I don't look like his son, I look like his twin! I instantly fell in love with him. "Dad, I'm sorry," I say over and over. "I didn't know."

Do I now have a new-found responsibility? Do I have a responsibility to forgive? Do I have a responsibility to ensure that this type of destruction never occurs again in my family? Do I have a responsibility of restoration?!

Hebrews 12:6–11 because the Lord disciplines those he loves, and he punishes everyone he accepts as a son." 7 Endure hardship as discipline; God is treating you as sons. For what son is not disciplined by his father? 8 If you are not disciplined (and everyone undergoes discipline), then you are illegitimate children and not true sons. 9 Moreover, we have all had human fathers who disciplined us and we respected them for it. How much more should we submit to the Father of our spirits and live! 10 Our fathers disciplined us for a little while as they thought best; but God disciplines us for our good, that we may share in his holiness. 11 No discipline seems pleasant at the time, but painful. Later on, however, it produces a harvest of righteousness and peace for those who have been trained by it. NIV

If you have not done so, you know of others that have thanked their parents for the chastisement received as a kid. This Scripture says your human fathers did it because you belonged to them, and you were not allowed to make them look bad. And, you respected them for it. After becoming a grownup you even thanked them. The Scripture is saying God chastised us, so that we may be in right standing with Him! Doesn't that give us a great responsibility as children of the Father of Lights?

Growing up, I remember hearing parents say, "You better behave yourself." The problem with that instruction is I don't recall them saying why you ought to behave yourself. If you had a half of a brain, you sort of figured out that there would be the obvious punishment if you didn't comply. Right?

Now, therein lies the problem. You want me to do something, but you're not going to explain to me why you want me to do it. If I am the child, I'll to do it because I'm obedient and don't want any trouble. But in most cases, we're going to find ourselves back in the same situation if you don't explain why I have to obey you.

Most parents understand when a child misbehaves, it's a direct reflection on the parenting skills of the parent. I have heard parents make comments like: "They learned that from their dad," or "They learned that from their mother." It's important for the son/daughter to clearly understand there is a responsibility to the parent for their training and care.

"I'm gonna cry!"

Once upon a time I was in a business office waiting room. There were people scattered throughout the room reading or just sitting. The room was quiet until in walks a mom with a two or three-year-old in tow. The entire room was immediately drawn to these two. They were putting on an academy award performance. The little fellow wanted something that Mom had already refused. Now, the little person was in a situation that he had obviously been in before, in public. He knew this quiet setting could be used to his advantage. He began to threaten his mom, "I'm gonna cry;

I'm gonna cry" Guess what? It worked! Mom gave the little fellow what he wanted, and his tactic was reinforced and assured to work the next time around.

How you behave is greatly influenced by who your parents are, especially your father.

Father: Pater one who has infused his own spirit into others, who actuates and governs their minds; one who stands in a father's place and looks after another in a paternal way; a title of honour; teachers, as those to whom pupils trace back the knowledge and training they have received; God is called the Father of the stars, the heavenly luminaries, because he is their Creator, Upholder, Ruler

It is fascinating to me how God made our minds to retain everything. He made us this way so that when we are taught something, we will always remember it. He made us that way so that we would follow in His ways.

> How you behave is greatly influenced by who your parents are, especially your father.

After Adam and Eve ate of the tree of the knowledge of good and evil, man did not lose the ability to retain everything. The problem with this composition, we remember the good and the evil.

—✦—

RONALD'S BEHAVIORAL TRAINING

Ronald's home was always filled with fighting and arguing by his grandmother, mother, and his three aunts: Lisa, Joann, and Olivia. He shared his first fifteen years of his life with five women that seemed to despise each other. Ronald would sit in his room listening to the arguing. "Are they really sisters?" he would think.

Once he was listening as his Aunt Lisa was hollering at his mom Betty, "I should have left you standing on the corner. I had thirty minutes to get to work and you knew it. Yet you took your sweet time coming out of the store. You are the dumbest woman on the planet. You have no sense of time Then you stood out front of the store talking to the other dumb, so-called friend of yours, while I'm waiting in my car like your chauffeur. I don't know how to tell you this Betty, except the truth. I hate your guts!"

There's a long silence. All of a sudden Ronald hears a loud crash coupled with a screaming sound coming from his mother. Betty was screaming as loud as possible, "I'll kill you. I'll kill you."

Ronald ran downstairs to find his mom sitting on top of Aunt Lisa's chest with her hands around her neck, choking her. Aunt Lisa had her hands wrapped around Betty's wrist struggling for her life. Ronald ran and lunged toward his mom like a football linebacker and knocked his mom off Aunt Lisa. All three lay on the floor for a few seconds that seemed like thirty minutes. Ronald slowly got up and looked down at the two ruffled opponents on the floor, both on their backs. Aunt Lisa was rubbing her neck crying. Ronald's mom Betty had her knees in the air with feet on the floor. Ronald shook his head in disgust and said, "I'm out of here."

Ronald had $217. saved in a sock hidden in a drawer in his room. He went to his room and packed a large backpack with a few clothes and personal items. Ronald had made up in his mind that he was leaving and had no idea where he was going.

As Ronald approached the front door to leave, he could hear the women in the kitchen continue to argue about who started the fight, what would happen the next time, back and forth back and forth. Their actions and arguing sealed the deal: Ronald would not go in and say goodbye. He quickly opened the door and disappeared into the shadows of the late evening.

Ronald found himself walking in the direction of the Greyhound bus station even though it was at least 10 miles from his house. As he walked, thoughts of his conversations with his father during the infrequent phone calls from prison danced in his head. His dad told him on several occasions if he ever needed anything to contact his brother Larry. Ronald's Uncle Larry was the one that took him to the ballgames when he was small. Ronald always reflected on the good times at the ballpark with Uncle Larry. Then Uncle Larry got married, and he and Aunt Sarah began to have baby after baby like they were in competition with another family. Uncle Larry would always check up on Ronald, never forgot his May 19th birthday, and said if he ever needed anything to call him. Ronald always remembered Uncle Larry's phone number because it ended with the same numbers as Ronald's birthday 0519.

When Ronald reached the bus station, it was late and his feet felt as if they had blisters on the bottom. Ronald went inside the dimly lit station that was a large room with church pews lined in the center. His eyes fell on what was probably the only pay phone in the entire city in the back of the station across from the restrooms. Uncle Larry. Ronald got change from the overweight man at the ticket counter and dropped the coins in the pay phone to call Uncle Larry. Ronald began to slowly push each number of Uncle Larry's phone number as if he were unsure if he would proceed to the next number. He made it to the last number as if he were surprised that he remembered it. After one ring Aunt Sarah answered the phone as if she were waiting for Ronald's call, but her surprised voice let Ronald know she wasn't expecting him. After pleasantries she gave the phone to Uncle Larry.

"What's up sport?" Uncle Larry answered.

Ronald explained what happened with his mother and aunt that day. Before he could continue, Uncle Larry interrupted, "I want you to come live with us. I don't want you at that rat hole anymore. Where are you?" Uncle Larry blurted. Ronald purchased his ticket and boarded the bus that began his 123 mile journey to his new life with his uncle.

There was little to no resistance from Ronald's mom of the new living arrangements. After all, Betty knew that Larry had always been good to Ronald and for him. For the next four years Ronald learned a new lifestyle. He learned what it meant to have a real family in a home with lots of love. Uncle Larry, along with his wife Sarah, taught Ronald the meaning of the father and opened him to a whole new way of living. Ronald learned the responsibility of having a dad in his life. His new dad was used to put him on an entirely different path.

(The story and characters have been created from years of counseling and do not represent any individuals present or past.)

In the illustration above, the character Ronald was presented with two different lifestyles.

> The first act of sin in the world was separating the Father from His offspring.

There is a responsibility from the child to the parent and the parent to child regarding behavior.

The first act of sin in the world was separating the Father from His offspring.

It is the ploy of the enemy to keep you from your father. Adam and Eve had a responsibility in having God as their Father. You know how that worked out.

Genesis 2:25 And they were both naked, the man and his wife, and were not ashamed.

Genesis 3:7-8 Then the eyes of both of them were opened, and they knew that they were naked; and they sewed fig leaves together and made themselves coverings. 8 And they heard the sound of the LORD God walking in the garden in the cool of the day, and Adam and his wife hid themselves from the presence of the LORD God among the trees of the garden.

Genesis 3:11 And He said, "Who told you that you were naked? Have you eaten from the tree of which I commanded you that you should not eat?"

In today's vernacular, God probably would have said, "Ah man. You've been talking to someone other than Me. I didn't tell you that you were naked. This changes our entire relationship!"

Sin opened their eyes. When you walk with God, you walk by hearing, not by sight. God is your eyes. You don't need eyes, so to speak. You need your spirit to be in tune with His Spirit for His leading.

Eve was able to see that the tree was good to eat prior to eating it. But, they had been told not to eat from that tree. The Father had a reason for His instruction and warning. Here is the importance of the trust in the relationship. She had a responsibility to protect her relationship with the Father. Her desire for the food turned to lust for the food. Lust is accelerated desire. Her association with the serpent and her lack of responsibility to her relationship with the Father caused her to take the fruit.

When you have an understanding of the relationship that you have with the Father, you have a responsibility to protect that relationship. There is not much difference between natural and spiritual father. It is not difficult for the wrong voices, which we've discussed, to poison your relationship with your dad, regardless of which dad it is. But your relationship with Father God is to have such a lofty place in your heart that all measures are used to protect that union.

Look again at Genesis 3:7 Then the eyes of both of them were opened, and they realized they were naked; so they sewed fig leaves together and made coverings for themselves.

> The task of the enemy is to have you focus on what you don't have.

Man was now able to see what his needs were and began to provide for himself, rather than God providing for him,

"Who told you that you were naked?"

"Well look-a-there, you're naked and yo daddy ain't provided you no clothes. What kinda daddy you got?" That seed has to be planted in the mind of the human. It is the nucleus of the plan of the destruction of mankind. If you can be deceived to make accusations against the One that created you, the plan to avert your destiny is assured.

The task of the enemy is to have you focus on what you don't have. It causes you to hide. Dad has you focus on what you do have. That's intrinsic; it causes you to be affirmed. Regardless of what you have on the outside, Dad says what you have on the inside far exceeds the exterior.

The enemy's job is to get you to question what your Father has said to you in order to bring doubt. Then, he wants you to focus on what God did not say. His mission is to get you to accept what he (the devil) is saying instead of what God has said. That same ploy is used with natural and spiritual dads. It works.

We've been looking at this dad thing all wrong.

1. Something that was inside of my dad (seed) caused me to be what I am.

2. Something inside of Father God (His love) caused me to be what I am.

3. Something inside of my spiritual dad (experience/love/destiny) caused me to be what I am.

4. You have a responsibility to that. Thanks Dad, Dad, especially You Dad.

Place a pause right here and understand the responsibility we have to our Father for being.

The very essence of who Father God, natural father, and spiritual father is, is to CAUSE TO BE. When we understand that, we take our responsibility to defend His/his position. Not as the enemy of our souls has done so well in his plan. We now live in a culture where the position of father is not just misunderstood, there is a fight to destroy it. But since it can't be destroyed, at least not for now, scientists are working feverishly to produce man in tubes. So, for now, the culture is saying father your job is to create. Then we'll take it from there.

Genesis 3:22 And the LORD God said, "The man has now become like one of us, knowing good and evil. He must not be allowed to reach out his hand and take also from the tree of life and eat, and live forever."

If man had remained in the garden and ate of the other tree, it would have further alienated him from his relationship with Father God! If man knows good and evil, he knows how to provide for himself. AND he lives forever. Then, what does he need God for? We see it in our culture today. Man is on a never ending quest to live forever. Mankind is becoming smarter and smarter on the way to live longer and longer. Entire industries have been created to teach people how to live forever. There is absolutely nothing wrong with living healthy, in fact, it's biblical. However, the goal of the enemy of our souls is not health, it is destruction.

Malachi 4:6 And he will turn The hearts of the fathers to the children, And the hearts of the children to their fathers, Lest I come and strike the earth with a curse.

The main reason Jesus came was to restore the relationship of the Father and child. We focus too much on salvation without explaining what salvation is. We sell salvation as fire insurance. It's relationship. Do you get fire insurance? Yes. But it's a fringe benefit, not the entire package.

The product Jesus sold was a relationship with the Father. How far removed are we from that message today? The message of discipleship is to BE like your Dad. Then, go and show others how to be like Him. Our natural dads and spiritual dads teach that as well. Be like me. Now, go into the world and behave like I taught you.

Thanks, Dad.

LET THE HEALING BEGIN

This book means so much to me. In that, I've been afforded with a premium of the best of the best in the father university. I owe so much to my dads. Yet, as I've walked the planet, nation after nation, my heart has ached as I've seen the lack of fathers, and even worst, the lack of understanding of the father.

> You can truthfully say it is synonymous to be a prisoner and fatherless.

Years ago, my first visit to a prison tore my heart apart. It was the beginning of a prosperous ministry to the incarcerated. As I took the long drive up North Interstate-65, I had no idea what I was entering. I exited the designated ramp and made a left turn to cross the bridge over the highway. As I approached the other side, the sight caused my mouth to drop. On one side of the road there was a sea of cattle. I don't remember ever seeing that many cows grouped together like that. Before I could digest that scene, I looked on the other side and there was a beautiful herd of horses. I love horses.

As I drove on, I realized by the signs that it was all owned by the government. As this whole scene was being downloaded in my head, the three prisons sprang up on the canvas. The one I was going to was on the left. Oh, I was not prepared for this a sea of black men all dressed in white prison garb. A herd of cattle. A herd of horses. Now, a herd of black men. I confess, that day I cried. I never cried like that before. The tears were falling like a broken levee, with no sound. That day a part of me died.

The amount of prisoners that are fatherless is astounding. You can truthfully say it is synonymous to be a prisoner and fatherless.

- 63% of youth suicides are from fatherless homes (Source: U.S. D.H.H.S., Bureau of the Census

- 90% of all homeless and runaway children are from fatherless homes

- 85% of all children that exhibit behavioral disorders come from fatherless homes (Source: Center for Disease Control)

- 80% of rapists motivated with displaced anger come from father-less homes (Source: Criminal Justice & Behavior, Vol 14, p. 403-26, 1978.)

- 71% of all high school dropouts come from fatherless homes (Source: National Principals Association Report on the State of High Schools.)

- 75% of all adolescent patients in chemical abuse centers come from fatherless homes (Source: Rainbows for all God's Children.)

- 70% of juveniles in state-operated institutions come from father-less homes (Source: U.S. Dept. of Justice, Special Report, Sept 1988)

- 85% of all youths sitting in prisons grew up in a fatherless home (Source: Fulton Co. Georgia jail populations, Texas Dept. of Corrections 1992)

Whose responsibility is it to restore the relationship of the father and the child? Whose responsibility is it to stop the cycle of no fathers? With the rise of no fathers, we've had the rise of homosexuality. Who is responsible to teach fatherhood? Moms? No.

For the healing to be done,

(This list is not to belittle the great organizations that are doing awesome work in all of the following. This is a call for others to join the effort.)

Men that understand fatherhood must rise up. There must be an all hands on deck urgency to restore the relationship of father/child.

The makeup of family must be calibrated to include those who are fatherless.

The error of homosexuality must be approached with showing loving fatherhood, not condemnation of sin.

Adoption with papers is not needed as much as adoption of the heart. Fathers must open their hearts, their homes, and give their time and their money to eliminate fatherlessness.

Those that have had great dads in their life must take a greater lead in perpetuating the life of their father through others.

There must be a true vision casting by those that understand the restoration of who the father is in the life of the offspring.

There needs to be a refuting of the movie makers that make the father look stupid and unnecessary in cartoons and commercials.

There is a great need for prayer and intercession specifically for the restoration of the father/child relationship.

There is a great need for pastors and spiritual leaders to create an atmosphere of the love of the Father.

DAD SAID,

I am the Way, the Truth, and the Life. No one comes to the Father except through me.

- Jesus Christ

I cannot think of any need in childhood as strong as the need for a father's protection.

- Sigmund Freud

My father used to say that it's never too late to do anything you wanted to do. And he said, "You never know what you can accomplish until you try."

- Michael Jordan

It is easier for a father to have children than for children to have a real father.

- Pope John XXIII

When you have a good mother and no father, God kind of sits in. It's not enough, but it helps.

- Dick Gregory

I imagine God to be like my father. My father was always the voice of certainty in my life. Certainty in the wisdom, certainty in the path, certainty always in God. For me God is certainty in everything. Certainty that everything is good and everything is God.

- Yehuda Berg

Then, there is Herbert Richey, circa 1906. As I approached my 1963 Volkswagen that I had driven to the job site, I noticed he'd found the protection that I thought was hidden. He's resting in the driver's seat, door open, facing outward with his feet on the ground.

"Boy, a man can go to bed with a lot of women and be wore out by the time he's thirty. Or, he can get married to one woman and have sex forever and be strong."

- Herbert J. Richey

Thanks, Dad.